An Irish Face

Maura O'Sullivan

An Irish Face

Maura O'Sullivan

As told to and edited by
Angela Keane

Story Preserves
Denver, Colorado

Copyright © 2012 Angela Keane
All rights reserved, including the right of reproduction in whole or in part in any form. Permission is granted to copy or reprint portions for any noncommercial use.

ISBN-13: 978-1453869451
ISBN-10: 145386945X

Library of Congress Control Number: 2011940822

BISAC Category:
Biography & Autobiography / Personal Memoirs

First edition

Story Preserves
Denver, Colorado
storypreserves@gmail.com

Maura and I began this project together in 2006. Sandwiched in between time spent with our families, friends, and other day-to-day activities, we talked about what life was like for Maura to grow up in Ireland, move to England, and live most of her adult life in America.

From our conversations, letters Maura saved along with other memorabilia including an audio tape she recorded after watching the movie, The Magdalene Sisters, *and a video recorded by her daughter Zana, I pieced together this narrative of her life using Maura's voice (as I heard it) wherever possible.*

The snippets taken from Jack's letters to Maura have been reproduced as he wrote or typed them, and have been edited for clarity and brevity only.

IT CAN BE a daunting and time consuming task to capture the stories that make up one's life. It's impossible to record all the events, let alone remember most of them, so why bother trying? Lynn Lauber, author of Listen to Me: Writing Life into Memory says, "Writing out of your life is a fine method of bequeathment, a way of handing down what you've lived and known, of reaching out a hand in kinship across time."

My hope is this book inspires the readers to capture their own family stories in writing, on audio, or video—whichever works best—so future generations have a better understanding of what it is to be a member of their clan.

For
Mary O'Sullivan
of
Caheragh Parish
1891-1955

Maura sightseeing in London with Jack
Summer of 1955

This one of you I really like. You look pure Irish. I guess thats because you are.

(Jack's comments on the back of the picture)

Saturday, September 6th, 2003. I've been to see the movie, *The Magdalene Sisters*. I knew enough not to see it alone because I knew it would affect me, but I didn't realize it would affect me like this. Good God, I'm 68 years old, and I still don't understand what makes me tick.

If I'd been born in China or Afghanistan or anywhere else in the world, I'd still be the same person I am right now. I believe that. But who am I anyway? I remember thinking one time that I was just Irish. That was the only thing I knew, and that was good enough. I love Ireland, and I love being Irish. It doesn't matter who gave me the genes I have. I can accept Ireland as my parents better than any humans. That I am a daughter of Ireland is the most steady and solid part of me.

Why am I crying? I'd like to know.

The circumstances of my conception have nothing to do with it—I wasn't there, but depending on what family you are born into, everything happens from there.

I was born, unwanted of course, and that troubled me—that I was unwanted. But then I had to be grateful. That was the worst part of it. I had to be grateful. And sometimes even as a child I'd wonder why *I* had to be grateful. Nobody else I knew had to be grateful. I'm not talking about being thankful for what your parents did for you; I was supposed to be grateful someone bothered to take me in, and I just didn't feel all that grateful.

It was a good thing I didn't look like anyone else in my family because my behavior wasn't blamed on that. (You awful thing, you're just like so and so....) I was spared those kinds of comparisons, and even at a very young age, I was thankful for that. But because I didn't feel grateful for the right things, I knew I wasn't a good person. Maybe that contributes to it, but it's not why I feel bad now.

Do I feel sorry for myself? No, that's not it. I'm really proud of who I am and where I've been. I don't feel sorry for me.

Where is all this emotion coming from? What exactly am I feeling? I'm holding back the tears, but why? I've always been that way—holding back. I've had a tough life. Big deal. My life isn't any tougher than anybody else's.

So what is my sad story?

Part One

Ireland

"They have no rights," I said. "Once they enter the gates they lose all rights about themselves, their bodies, their souls, and also all rights to their babies or their whereabouts."

> June Goulding, *The Light in the Window*, (Great Britain: Ebury Press, 2005), 194. [A memoir written about Goulding's work as a midwife at Sacred Heart in Bessboro during the 1950s.]

An Irish Face

That I was born in a convent had more to do with who got my mother pregnant than that she was pregnant. She gave birth to me at Sacred Heart Convent in Bessboro, outside the city of Cork. We just called it Bessboro. One had to have money to give birth in a convent, and she didn't have it, so it must have been the one who got her pregnant that did.

Ireland

Women who gave birth outside of marriage and without the means to hide their pregnancies in a convent raised their children in poverty under a blanket of shame and whispers directed at them and their children because of their mother's unmarried status.

According to my birth certificate, the woman who gave birth to me on 11 February 1935 worked as a maid. Women in her day could be teachers, nurses, shop girls, or maids; that was about it. My older sister, Annie, told me my original mother worked as a maid in a doctor's home when she got pregnant. Annie thought the doctor was my father, but my cousin heard the doctor's son was responsible for my birth. Whoever my father was, he must have paid for her keep. In order for my mother to stay in the convent until I was born, someone had to pay because there was no money from the government for that sort of thing, and the nuns wouldn't have taken her without pay.

What was the story there? I'll probably never know but the story begins there.

I was born like anybody else, but because of the circumstances of my birth, I was different. This was something I could never discuss with the woman who raised me. What little I know, I pieced together from bits and pieces that were told to me at various times over the years.

The story of my birth was never discussed while I was growing up. Nobody told me I was adopted, but everybody (including me) knew it. We pretended it didn't happen. There was this big lie attached to me the whole time I was growing up. I wasn't really even adopted; I was a "nursing child." Not until I was married with four daughters of my own, did Mother tell me she had met the woman who gave birth to me.

Unlike some of the pregnant girls at the convent, my first mother was allowed to leave after my birth. In fact, she was on the bus when Mother took me to live with her in Cork. According to Mother, "She didn't say much; she was a cold and distant woman."

What that five mile ride to Cork City was like for Mary O'Sullivan—seeing her child for the last time in the arms of a stranger—I'll never know.

WHEN I WAS BORN, children of unwed mothers were fostered out to "nursing mothers." My nursing mother, Mary Moore, was given a monthly allowance to help take care of me until I was three years old. After that, she was expected to care for me for God's reward. I learned how it all worked when I was 13 years old, and Mother brought my new baby sister, Angela, home from Bessboro.

Ireland

Adoption was not legal in Ireland until 1952.[1] When Irish adoption laws changed, adoptions became retroactive automatically for some of the children fostered out as nursing children. Angela, who was born in 1948, was included in the provision; I was not.

AT A VERY EARLY AGE, before I understood that Mother was not the one who gave birth to me, my friends and I were discussing how babies were born, and it was a mystery to me that my mother didn't have a husband and hadn't had one for many years, but nevertheless she was still my mother.

Mother treated me no better or worse than she did her two biological daughters, Annie and Kittie, but even so, I knew I was different from them. I heard whispers, a secret everyone knew but didn't share with me.

One day when I was young, as I clung to my mother while she visited with another woman, the

---

[1] "The Catholic Church, exerting a tremendous influence on the legislature of the Republic of Ireland, apposed legal adoption even though the Catholic Church didn't disapprove of it in other countries. The fear in Ireland was that Protestants would take Catholic babies and raise them in the Protestant religion. If adoptions were legalized, there would be no way to get those babies back into the One True Faith."
J. H. Whyte, *Church & State in Modern Ireland, 1923-1979*, (Gill and Macmillan, 1980), 191.

woman asked my mother if I was her child. I looked up in time to see Mother mouthing the words, "nursing child." Another time my friend Breda Desmond overheard her family talking about me, and she told me I was a nursing child. I pretended she was telling me old news.

When I went home, I asked Mother, "What's a nursing child?"

"How did you hear that?" she asked.

When I told her it came from Breda, she got very angry and said what a horrible child Breda was for telling me this. She never explained what a nursing child was or why it shouldn't be talked about.

I OFTEN WONDERED what my first mother was like. I would dream about her coming to reclaim me from the Moore family. She was rich, of course, and she would bring me expensive clothes and other nice presents. These fantasies made me feel ungrateful and disloyal to the mother I had because even though it wasn't easy living with Mother, I still loved her.

I wasn't so sure Mother loved me because she was mad at me all the time. It wasn't just me; she was angry with everyone. Mother could hardly read or write, but she was smart and ambitious. She was always in search of money. Among her siblings, she had the least education and went to work at the earliest age. Her siblings, as well as her children, feared her as much as they loved her. Nobody could have the upper hand with Mother. She thought herself better than everyone and said so often.

MOTHER BROUGHT ME home from Bessboro on the bus to a house full of women besides herself: her mother, Annie McCale, who died when I was a baby; Biddie McCale, Mother's unmarried sister; and Mother's two biological daughters, Annie and Kittie.

Mother's husband, Jeremiah (Jerry) Moore left Ireland before I joined the family. He was older than Mother and had been a soldier with the IRA during the "troubles." When he immigrated to America and wanted Mother to join him, she told him she couldn't leave Ireland because her mother needed her (even though she had siblings who could have looked after their mother.) I think Mother stayed in Ireland because she wanted to, not because she had to.

Jerry remained in America and Mother in Ireland, but they never dissolved their marriage, and Jerry eventually died in New York. When word got back to Mother that he was deceased, she applied for and received his social security benefits until her death in 1979 at the age of 76.

I LOVED MOTHER and I needed her, but I didn't feel safe with her. A painful memory I have from my early years was a day when I was running around the house laughing and making noise with another child about the same size as me. It was a warm summer day; all the doors and windows were open. Mother was working in the kitchen, preparing a meal for us, and she yelled at me to be quiet. Then she said, and I'll never forget her words, "I'd of been better off if I'd reared a pig."

It stunned me. I was small, no more than four or five years old, and I stopped immediately. I didn't understand exactly what she meant at the time, but I'll never forget how it made me feel. She couldn't have hurt me more if she'd knocked me to the ground.

WHEN I WAS QUITE young, Mother took me on vacation, just the two of us. This trip was something of a mystery to me because I was too young to know how it happened or where we were going, but we stayed in a hotel by the ocean for several days. It isn't a fond memory really; it was just something different I experienced. Mother didn't enjoy our time together; I remember her fussing at me the entire time. According to her, I couldn't even play in the water correctly.

I have no memory of Mother hugging me or praising me for anything. It always felt like I was a

Ireland

burden, just one more thing she had to deal with in her life. I never felt like I brought her joy, even the times when she bought me something. Once she purchased some new ribbons for me, but even that memory is tainted by her harsh remarks as she braided my hair. "Stop fidgeting and hold still so I can get this done."

Mother often said that God was going to reward her for being so good to me. I feel ungrateful for saying this, but I never felt she was especially good to me. She took me in and then left my care to her sister. When Aunt Biddie married and moved out, my sisters, Annie and Kittie, who were 12 and 13 years older than me, took care of me and gave me what mothering I had. As a very young child, I was left alone a lot. Not out of punishment or neglect, but because my mother and sisters were out working every day, and as soon as I was old enough to do so, I joined them.

How was God going to reward Mother? After she'd had a few drinks, she'd say that I was going to take care of her in her old age, which would be her reward from God. I didn't take care of her at the end of her life, so I turned out to be a total failure according to her expectations.

MY BIGGEST REGRET from childhood was my lack of education. Mother didn't consider schooling important for any of her daughters. If we were needed for something else that involved making money, it always took precedence. She was from the generation that didn't go to school because the schools at that time were run by the English, and a great number of Irish refused education because they feared being converted to Protestantism. As poor and impoverished as the Irish were, Catholicism was very important to them.

What little education I had was because Mother didn't want to face the fires of hell for not making sure I received the instructions for First Holy Communion and Confirmation in the Catholic Church.

Maura in front of St. Mary's Cathedral

Ireland

THE ONLY PICTURE that survived my childhood is the one taken on the day of my Confirmation. I wore a coat the town dressmaker fashioned from a grownup's discarded coat.

If it weren't for Mother's insistence on religious training, I probably wouldn't have learned to read and write at all. As it was, I barely learned the basics. I missed so much school that when I did go, I hated it. I would show up in the middle of a new lesson and wouldn't have any idea what was going on.

To the surprise of my teachers, because I did so poorly in all the other classes, the one thing I excelled at was religion class.

On Confirmation Day each child was given a card with their name and their parents' names on it. The children were all going around showing each other their cards, comparing their fathers' names and mothers' maiden names. Someone asked to see my card, but I didn't have one.

Just before I walked up the isle to be confirmed, a nun handed me my card and whispered to me that I wasn't supposed to look at it. I don't know what was on it, probably just my real name and my original mother's name.

I went by the last name Moore as it was the custom to assume the name of your foster family. I knew I had a different name; it just was never used.

An Irish Face

If you asked questions the adults didn't want to answer, you were called a busy body or a nosy parker[2]. I don't know where the expression comes from, but calling someone a nosy parker was one of many ways used to teach children they were to be seen not heard.

We lived in Gurranabraher, County Cork. Gurran for short. The government built masses of new houses on the outskirts of Cork City to relieve the tenement houses in the inner city. Families paid rent according to their income. As families vacated the tenement houses and moved into Gurran, the tenement houses were torn down. When Mother brought me home as a baby from the convent, we lived in a two bedroom house on St. Anne's Street, at the very edge of the older buildings. We slept four to a bed, adults and children together, two of us with our heads at the top and the other two with their heads at the bottom.

---

[2] "One suggestion, put forward by Eric Partridge in his Dictionary of Slang and Unconventional English, was that the saying dates from the Great Exhibition in Hyde Park in 1851. Very large numbers of people attended the Exhibition, so there would have been lots of opportunities for peeping Toms and eavesdroppers in the grounds. The word parker has since medieval times been used for an official in charge of a park, a park-keeper…. But all this is the purest supposition. The evidence isn't on record, and the truth will probably never be found."

Michael Quinion, *World Wide Words*, www.worldwidewords.org/qa/qa-nos2.htm

Ireland

When I was ten, we moved to Mount Eden Road and lived in a three bedroom house that was luxurious compared to the tiny house we lived in before.

Mother and my two older sisters went to work every morning, and from a very early age Mother expected me to get up on my own, dress myself, and get to school on time. Since there was no one there to make sure I did, most of the time I didn't.

I stayed in bed as long as I wanted and then spent the day hanging out with friends in the neighborhood who also ditched school. We walked out into the country to play in the fields, picked blackberries in the bushes that grew wild around our development, played in the stacks of bricks brought in to build homes, jumped rope, kicked the can and hop scotched our way through most of our school days.

On one of the days I did attend school, the school inspector came around to our classroom and talked to my teacher. I was called to the front of the room, and he asked me why I was absent for so long. I proudly told him I had a job. I had no idea there was anything wrong with that.

Mother was the foreman in a chicken processing plant. When Breda Desmond and I were old enough, Mother put us to work sorting feathers. We were looking for a particular feather that was worth money; I think it was used to make hats. Those days at the chicken factory were long days for me. I remember getting very sleepy as I sorted the feathers.

Mother was notified by the school officials that she would have to go to court because of my missing school. She was furious. "It's your fault for opening your big mouth," she told me. "They might put you back in the convent. That'll teach you."

I cried hard and pretended I was scared, but secretly I thought it might be a good thing to live in the convent. I would learn to read and write if I lived there. Mother couldn't call me an "eejit" and slap me with the back of her hand if I lived in the convent. It might be more fun than living with the fear of Mother's anger and the guilt of not being grateful enough.

After seeing the movie, *The Magdalene Sisters,* I'm not so sure. Except for the education I would have gotten, life in the convent would probably have been no better than life with Mother.

Despite how hard Mother and the rest of us worked, it was a struggle to make ends meet. There were times when we had nothing to eat in the house—not even a scrap of bread—just some old stuff in the pot. There were times we lived on bread, butter and tea or mashed potatoes and milk. We went through spells of affluence too, but I never knew what made the difference.

Ireland

For a time we had a pet goat, and then we didn't. It just disappeared one day. That night at dinner when I mentioned how sad it was our goat had disappeared, everyone laughed. I felt bad they were laughing at me and wouldn't tell me what was so funny. Much later I learned we were eating the goat for dinner that night.

MOTHER TOOK IN lots of children through the years. She took them in for the money and God's reward. I don't know how these children came to us, but I remember a little girl named Ellen who lived with us until she was two. Her mother came to visit her every week until she married a friend of our family's and took Ellen to live with her. We also had a little boy who died a few weeks after he came to live with us. I don't remember why the boy lived with us or why he died.

The boy's grandmother visited us after he died. She was dressed nice, she spoke well, and I liked her. She was different from the women I knew who all wore black woolen shawls as part of their everyday clothes. They used the shawls to keep warm but also to carry things home from the market. When I was about seven or so, Mother wrapped me and a baby together in a shawl so I could carry the baby around without dropping her.

An Irish Face

THERE WERE NO BOOKS or magazines in our home, just the occasional newspaper. I was 12 years old when my friend Ellen O'Brien took me to a library for the first time. I didn't even know there were such places. I was amazed to see a building full of books you could borrow to read and not pay anything. I went home and told everyone about my discovery. No one at home knew about libraries either. My older sisters taunted me and made fun. "Who do you think you are?" they asked, but their friend Nonie who was at the house said, "I wish I could read."

One of the books I remember checking out of the library was *Pollyanna* by Eleanor H. Porter.

Mother's sister, Bridget (we called her Biddie) lived with us and took care of me until she married and moved into her own home. I loved the Sundays when Biddie and her family visited us.

Going to Biddie's house was like Sunday only better. Biddie could make something special out of nothing. She would take a worn out pair of discarded men's pants that were shiny in the thighs, cut out the good material and make a nice pair of pants for one of her three boys.

When I visited Biddie, and I did as often as I could, she was always glad to see me. For a treat she offered me a slice of buttered bread, and I felt as though she'd served me the finest piece of pound cake in all of Ireland.

Once when I was at Biddie's house, three young girls (older than me) stopped by to show Biddie their new dresses. They twirled around, showing off for Biddie, giggling as she oohed and aahed over them. When the girls left, Biddie worried she'd made me sad. She knew I didn't have any dresses like the ones we'd just seen, nor would I be getting any soon.

It was always a big deal to get a new dress as nobody had a lot of clothes back then and although I had a brand new First Communion dress, most of my clothing was purchased second hand. Once Mother found a jacket and skirt that was a suit kind of thing she purchased from another mother whose daughter had outgrown it. I'd seen her wear it; then I got to have it. It was a nice outfit, and it didn't bother me that I wasn't the first one to own it.

Biddie's concern for me took me by surprise. I wasn't sad at all watching Biddie make a big deal out of those pretty dresses. Watching Biddie shower the girls with compliments was something new to me, and I enjoyed seeing it. Listening to her kind and loving words was music to my ears.

Mother grew jealous of the time I spent at Biddie's house. "You're down there all the time. Why don't you stay home?" I couldn't explain it to Mother;

An Irish Face

it would only make her angry. She didn't forbid me to go, so I continued to visit Biddie as often as I could.

My two older sisters, Annie and Kittie, were 12 and 13 when I joined the family, and they were good to me. I would sometimes try to get their sympathy by saying, "Well, I'm just a nursing child," but they didn't let me get away with much. Annie and Kittie were so much more grown up than I was, it was fun to be "a fly on the wall" when they hung out with their friends. The kindness of my sisters balanced things out for me. Mother just wasn't a hugging, kissing, kind of woman; holding babies was the kindest thing I ever saw her do.

I WAS 13 WHEN we picked up my little sister, Angela, from Bessboro. Annie and Kittie were both married and raising children of their own by then.

Annie was pregnant with her daughter, Mary, when Mother saw an advertisement in the paper for a baby in Bessboro who needed a nursing mother. She took me with her to the agency to convince them she was capable of caring for a child, but she never said a word to me about what she was doing.

Over the years I'd learned not to ask questions. Find your place and stay there. Just go along if you don't want to be told, "Shut up, it's none of your business."

I sat quietly as Mother talked. At one point in the

conversation, she pointed to me and whispered to the woman in charge that the fine girl sitting next to her was her nursing child.

I hated it when she called me a "fine girl." The way she said it made me feel like a big ugly thing.

Throughout the interview no one asked me anything or bothered to check me out, and it was decided that Mother was qualified to raise another Bessboro child. So next we went to the convent to pick up the baby.

There were two babies at the convent that day, and the nuns brought both of them for us to look at. Mother turned to me and asked which one I liked best.

I felt awful. It was the worst question I'd ever been asked. This was so like my beginning and I knew that, but I couldn't explain what I was feeling; nobody wanted to hear it anyway. How could I choose one baby over another? I wanted no part of that decision.

I said something (not nice) to Mother, and she got very angry with me. The two nuns just stood there holding the babies while Mother scolded me. Finally Mother picked the baby that would become my little sister, Angela. When we left the convent, a woman watched us from the window on the second floor. Mother motioned to her, is this your baby? The woman nodded, yes.

Her legal name was Mary Angela, but we called

her Angela. I loved taking care of her. When her crying was too much for Mother, I'd console her as my aunt and sisters had done for me when I was a baby. Mother was much kinder to Angela than she was to Annie, Kittie, or me, which was a good thing because two years after Angela joined our family, I left for England with Annie and her husband, Doland Desmond.

Angela and Mother

ANGELA BECAME the focus of Mother's life; she was devoted to her. Years later when Kit (Annie's daughter) got married, she wanted to get dressed in

Ireland

Angela's room, but Mother didn't want anyone to use her bedroom. Someone had to intervene so Kit had a place to dress for her wedding.

At one point Angela was engaged to a young Irish man, but Mother didn't like him, and she chose not to marry him. Angela never married and eventually moved to Spain with her cousin Mary (Annie's daughter who is the same age as Angela.) The two of them have remained friends all their lives.

In 1950 while Annie and Doland were still married to each other, they came home for Christmas to visit their children: Brenda, Kit, and Mary who stayed in Ireland with Mother while they worked in Birmingham. (Jerry was born later in England as well as Timmy and Patrick, the children Annie had with her second husband, Timothy O'Callaghan.)

When Annie and Doland returned to England, my cousin Bridie Dennehey and I joined them. Because of the labor laws, I would not be allowed to work full time in England until I was 18 so I borrowed Bridie's sister's birth certificate. Though I was only 15 at the time, I was big for my age, and people told me I looked 18. I knew I'd have no trouble passing for an older girl.

It was no big deal to borrow my cousin's name. In Ireland, babies were commonly named after someone else in the family, and many people went by names other than their formal names. My Aunt Bridget was Biddie, my sister Kathleen was called Kittie, and though I was named Mary, I was called Maura.

As a child once, I snuck a peek at the teacher's book and saw my name written: Maura (O'Sullivan) Moore. I never said anything because the name O'Sullivan was one of the secrets I wasn't supposed to know about.

I was eager to be out from under Mother's thumb, off to a new country to experience new adventures, and if it took a new name to get there, so be it.

For the next few years in England I would answer to the name, Ellen Dennehey.

Part Two

England

Rationing continued after the end of the war in 1945, although the basic petrol ration for civilians was restored when peace returned. Indeed, some aspects of rationing actually became stricter for some years after the war.... Sweet rationing ended in February 1953, and sugar rationing ended in September 1953. However, the end of all food rationing was not until 4 July 1954, with meat the last to go.

http://en.wikipedia.org/wiki/Rationing_in_the_United_Kingdom

An Irish Face

I learned early on to live in the moment. At the age of 15, I changed my name to Ellen Dennehey and moved to England. I never used my real name anyway so why not be Ellen Dennehey for awhile? No problem, except I didn't like the name, Ellen. Nelly (which is what we called Bridie's sister) was much nicer sounding. A friend I met in England called me Helen for awhile because she liked it better than Ellen.

England

I had lived a lie for so many years that none of this bothered me a bit. Ellen's birth certificate served me well until a couple of years later when I tried to use my new identity to obtain a job in America.

My cousin, Bridie, got homesick almost immediately and returned to Ireland shortly after we arrived in Birmingham. I was expecting England to look more like what we knew about America through the movies and instead found architecture similar to Ireland's. Even though England was a bit of a disappointment to me, I had no intention of going back home.

Housing was scarce. Doland stayed in a boarding house for men while Annie and I shared a room in another boarding house for women.

I was always a good worker and never had trouble finding jobs and keeping them, but I was limited to what kind of jobs I could apply for because of my lack of education. I worked with Annie in a factory making bathroom faucets and sinks for awhile. We dipped the faucets in chemicals, and after they soaked for a period of time, we rinsed them off and put them in more chemicals before they were passed on to the next person to work on.

After about six months of living and working in Birmingham, Annie found a room she could share with Doland. When she moved out, I shared my room with an older woman for awhile. When she left the boarding house, I moved to a smaller room for one person. It was the first time in my life I'd had that much space to myself, and I loved it.

While I was living at the boarding house, Annie went back to Ireland for some family reason; I no longer remember what it was. Doland was gone too, whether it was back to Ireland or somewhere else to work, I'm not sure. Except for Doland's younger brother Thomas, who also lived in Birmingham, I lived in a room by myself all alone in a city far away from home. I felt quite grown up with my very own ration book and wasn't the least bit homesick.

EVERY SATURDAY MORNING I sent money home to Mother by telegram, at least a pound, maybe thirty shillings (a pound and a half.) It was important that I send the money by telegram rather than through the mail. People watched the telegram boy coming down the street wondering which house he would stop at. Mother liked that.

A YOUNG MAN named Ronnie Griffith worked at the plumbing factory in another department. On my days off, I went to the movies or just walked around town. Everywhere I went I saw Ronnie Griffith. I'd go to the movies, look around, and he'd be sitting next to me. If I was walking down the street I'd see him on the other side of the street walking the same direction I was going. I didn't realize until later he was stalking me. We ended up dating for a bit and even talked about getting married, but I didn't want to be married so I broke it off.

Barely 16 years old, I lived in one room and shared the use of a kitchen and bathroom. What a pitiful life. But it wasn't pitiful to me. It felt full of possibilities. I was waiting for something to happen. I didn't know what it was I was waiting for, but it wasn't for what happened next.

Mother moved to London and wanted me to come and live with her and Angela. Kittie's husband, Dennis Earl worked in London and when he'd saved enough money he sent for Kittie and their children, Delia and Mary Anne, to join him. (Michael, Dennis, and Patrick were all born later in England.)

Because it was hard to find places to live, Kittie's family, Mother, and Angela all crowded together in two small rooms. Mother was on the list to rent rooms next to Kittie and Dennis. If I moved to London and got a job there, I could live with Mother and Angela and help with the rent on the new rooms.

While I was visiting the family in London, Mother talked me into quitting my job in Birmingham. I loved living by myself and didn't want to leave

An Irish Face

Birmingham, but because Mother wanted me to come to London, I went.

IN LONDON, I found a job cleaning rooms and making beds at a hospital that specialized in eye care. The hospital provided room and board for me as well as a small salary. With the money I gave Mother, she and Angela were able to move into the rooms next to Kittie and her family while I lived at the hospital.

Working and living at the hospital turned out to be more fun than living on my own in Birmingham. There were a number of girls my age living and working there, and it felt like I was living in a college sorority. We spent hours talking and laughing together. Most of the girls were Irish, but some were German and Welsh. The Irish girls tended to pick on each other and trade insults. One girl from County Cork tried to befriend me, but when she insulted me I hauled off and whacked her. We never spoke again. Mostly though I got along with people. The patients and nurses I worked with liked me. One day I was talking to a nurse, and she told me that the sun shining through my hair made it look like it was on fire. It was rare enough that anyone in my family ever told me I looked nice, so when I did get a compliment, I remembered it.

England

On our evenings off, we went to dances and flirted with boys. To impress the guys we told them we were nurses at the hospital. I suppose I was attractive enough because I didn't have any trouble finding guys to dance with, but I didn't care for most of them. I was in search of love and romance, but most of them were just interested in getting physical.

I remember one of the girls in our group came home from a date one night, hysterical, because her boyfriend asked her to marry him. We finally got it out of her, "I think I said yes."

ALTHOUGH SOME PEOPLE in London owned televisions at that time, my first exposure to it was after the death of King George VI, the Queen Mum's husband. He died in his sleep at the age of 56. On 6 February 1952 the funeral was televised, and a bunch of us got permission to watch it in the conference room at the hospital. We sat on the floor, gathered around a tiny television set. It was a bad screen—very snowy—but you could still see what was going on, and we were fascinated by the whole experience.

THREE OF MY FRIENDS and I decided we were going to get jobs as domestic help and move to America. Our plan was to work for one year with a family then spend the next four years traveling the

An Irish Face

United States together. We would live for one month in each of the 48 states before we moved on to the next one. We spent hours in our rooms at the hospital drilling each other on the names of the states and talking about all the things we were going to do when we got to America.

Because I was still shy of my 18th birthday, I applied to go to America as Ellen Dennehey. What a commotion I caused! When the police visited Ellen (who still lived in Ireland), the family thought they were in trouble. The authorities asked why Ellen Dennehey wanted to go to American and she said, "I want to do no such thing."

That brought a detective from Scotland Yard to the hospital to interview the Ellen Dennehey imposter. When I learned there was a detective in the office who wanted to speak to me, I was terrified. I cried hysterically on the way to the office and couldn't stop crying throughout the interview. The detective was actually quite nice to me. He was somewhat amused by my coming to England under a false identity. He asked me, "What did you think you'd find when you got here, the streets paved with gold?"

The interview with the detective was the extent of the trouble I got into posing as Ellen Dennehey, but it ended my plans to go to America with the other girls. Out of the four of us, only one of us actually went to

England

America at that time, and she came back after her year of service with a family. After she got back to London, I ran into her on the street, and we went into the pub for a drink and talk about her American adventure. That's how I looked at going to America at that time; it was an adventure I wanted to experience.

PEGGY SHERIDAN, one of the girls I tried to go to America with, became a great friend of mine. We lived together at the hospital for a year and a half. When Peggy went to visit her sister who also lived in London, she invited me to join her. On one of those visits I got just about the best compliment of my life. An older brother, who was also visiting their sister, saw me for the first time and said, "Now there's an Irish face!" Since I thought of Ireland as my missing parents, it felt good to know someone thought that of me.

Another sister of Peggy's had died, and Peggy's mother was raising her orphaned grandson in Cheltenham. Peggy's mother wanted Peggy to move back to Cheltenham and help her with the child. Peggy asked me to join her. At first I hesitated. I'd been writing to a Canadian sailor I'd met at one of the dances. He'd gone home to Canada but was making plans to come back to London to visit me. If I went with Peggy, I wouldn't get to see him.

On the other hand, there was an American Air Force Base next to the nearby town of Gloucester, and Peggy and I always had fun dancing with the Americans. I wrote to the Canadian and told him I was leaving London and I moved to Cheltenham with Peggy.

When I left London, I stopped giving money to Mother. (Some people I talked to thought I was giving Mother more of my salary than I should, but Mother didn't think so.) By this time I was older and felt more independent so I just stopped sending her money.

Mother probably still expected it, but I was about 100 miles away, and she couldn't call me on the telephone.

We had some money when we left London, so we took the train to Cheltenham and had a grand time in the dining car flirting with the young men who were on the train with us. Peggy and I found jobs right away at a hotel that catered to Americans, and we were given a room to share in the basement of the hotel.

I thought it was a great job, but Peggy didn't see it that way. The owner wanted us to clean her quarters and dust her shoes. Peggy wasn't about to dust anybody's shoes, and she told the woman so before she quit. Then Peggy talked me into quitting too. We didn't want to face the owner so we waited until night and snuck back into the hotel through the window to get our things.

England

I learned a lot from Peggy.

After our hotel job ended, we moved in with Peggy's mother. She lived in a small complex of 12 houses located five miles outside Cheltenham. These houses were temporary houses built very quickly after the war to accommodate folks until they could find permanent housing arrangements.

We needed new jobs so we went to the Department of Employment. The brewery was hiring people, but I said I didn't want to work there.

The woman helping me find work said, "You'd better rephrase that. When jobs are scarce, you don't turn one down just because you don't like it."

I confessed I couldn't stand the smell of the brewery.

"Now that's a good excuse," she said.

I got hired as a waitress, Peggy found work in a department store, and we continued to live the carefree life. We dated, went to dances, and laughed a lot.

On various occasions, Peggy and I hitchhiked to London for short visits. We had no fear of riding with strangers, so we stood by the bus stop near where we lived until a trucker heading for London stopped to pick us up. He'd then drop us off where we could take buses into the city. The truck drivers were delighted to have someone to talk to, and we were grateful for the free ride into London.

An Irish Face

I was shocked when one day Mother showed up in Cheltenham with Kittie's husband. I don't know how she talked Dennis into coming with her, but she did. Mother and Dennis came to Peggy's mother's house where we were staying at the time. Her mission was to get me to move back to London and help her and Angela. I didn't want to leave Cheltenham any more than I had wanted to leave Birmingham, but I did what I'd always done—what Mother wanted me to do.

I ASKED PEGGY to come back to London with me, and we worked together in a factory making shoulder pads. Shortly after we arrived in London, Peggy discovered she was pregnant and went back home as it wasn't a situation where she could marry the father of the baby. Mother was very judgmental about that sort of thing. When I was about 13 and still living with Mother in Ireland, one of my friends got pregnant, and Mother wouldn't let me see her anymore.

I was older now and could ignore Mother's disapproval of Peggy. We remained friends, and I visited Peggy once or twice after her child was born and brought presents for the baby. Even though she was unmarried, Peggy was delighted to be a mother.

Shortly after the birth of her daughter, she moved to Detroit to live with another sister who had moved there sometime earlier. I lost touch with her when she moved to America because I was too embarrassed of my writing to send letters to her.

Years later, Mother told me Peggy and her sister stopped by while on a visit to England to see if I lived in the same house. Mother was happy to tell them I lived in California.

"Didn't you give an address?" I asked.

She dismissed my question with a sound of disgust and waved her hand as though she couldn't be bothered.

MY SISTER KITTY and her family were living in two rented rooms in a large older home in London. Mother, Angela, and I rented two rooms in a similar house next door. Mother needed my income to help pay the rent. We had a sink half way up the stairs, but our bathroom and toilet were outside in the back yard. We used a bucket at night and emptied it in the morning in the outside toilet.

Our street was filled with big houses like those with rooms for rent after the war. Housing was scarce because of the bombings, and people took in boarders like us to help make ends meet.

I had a job in an advertising agency stuffing envelopes and other duties at that time. Mary McNally, a girl from the northern part of England, worked at the

An Irish Face

advertising agency with me, and we were great friends. Mary and I had fun together. Walking down the street, if Mary saw a man in front of us whose head looked attractive from the back, she'd run up to see if he was also good looking from the front.

Most of the young women we worked with were married. Mary and I listened to them discuss the silly things they told their husbands, and we were amazed. "Can you imagine if that's all you had to talk about?" We decided married life was terribly dull, and we were going to remain single. As bachelor girls, we would have apartments like Gene Kelly's in *American in Paris* with beds that pulled down from the wall. Mary even had "Bachelor Girl" cards made up with our names and addresses on them to carry in our wallets. I was now Maura Moore, B.G.

It was while I was working in the advertising agency that I met Jack Brown at a dance. He was stationed in Germany but came to London on holiday.

I REMEMBER IT was Election Day (26 May 1955), and the dance went on much longer than usual. When it ended, Jack walked me home. He took my number because he wanted to call me the next day but then lost the slip of paper he wrote it down on. He remembered where I worked, but not what I did, so he telephoned the agency and asked the receptionist on

England

each floor of the building if they had a beautiful Irish girl working there. I was so embarrassed when my supervisor told me some Yank was trying to get in touch with me by telephone.

We ended up spending a lot of time together the rest of the weekend, and when Jack left to go back to Germany, I promised I would write to him. I hated to write in those days. I still don't like to write, but at least now I understand why I am averse to putting pen to paper. I was always embarrassed by my lack of formal education, and I lived in fear of being found out by the mistakes I made.

Jack wrote to me constantly and insisted I write back. I did write to him, but not nearly as often or as long of letters as he wrote. I don't know what happened to my letters to Jack, but I kept his letters to me. I tucked them away and didn't look at them again until 2007 when I moved from my Littleton townhouse to my new home on Dry Creek Road.

I was glad I'd kept the letters. They reminded me why I fell in love with Jack in the first place.

9 June 1955
Dear Maura,
We finally got out of London but not as we expected. The airplane we were supposed to leave in was taken over by some generals. No other planes arrived that same day so we had to stay overnight and it just about cracked me up to know you were somewhere in London and I was so close. If it wasn't necessary for me to stay at the airport I would have come in and looked for you. For the first time since I've been in the Army I considered going AWOL.

I can't remember the last time I enjoyed myself as much as I did with you. The two days I was there and the time I was able to spend with you mean so much to me and I want very much to see you again. It may be possible. Keep your fingers crossed.

While growing up, Jack's family owned a farm his mother had inherited in Pennsylvania. The farm was located near a small village called Bingham Center, but his father didn't like farming, so when Jack was ten years old, his parents sold the farm and they moved to Olean, New York, a town close by.

Jack's family home in Olean was large and had carriage houses in the back that were converted to apartments. They lived on the first floor of the big house and rented out the rooms on the second floor.

England

Jack spent his grade school years studying in a one-room school house, but he went to high school in Olean and completed his high school education at the age of 16. Jack's father died of a heart condition when Jack was a teenager.

In the middle of his sophomore year of college at Syracuse, Jack dropped out to enlist in the army. He was drinking too much, not studying enough, and if he waited to be drafted, he would've had to serve two years. By enlisting he only had to serve 18 months.

23 June 1955

Dearest Maura,

Yesterday the company commander called me into his office and gave me a great shock. I thought I had done something wrong but after I had reported to him, he handed me a set of Corporal stripes and told me to put them on. So now I have one more stripe and an increase in pay. The latter I can really use.

Have you been dancing lately? Sure wish I could drop by the Lyceum this Friday night.

Hey just this minute I thought of a terrific idea. Why couldn't I call you at work some afternoon? I remember part of the number and I believe I could locate you easier now than I did before. If it is possible, tell me the number again (I remember the Museum part) and the department where you work.

An Irish Face

It was very hard for me to write letters because of my lack of schooling, but I did it anyway. I wasn't in love with Jack as much as he seemed to be with me, but I wanted to be. I didn't stay home worrying about it though. My home wasn't the kind you wanted to spend time in. There was nothing to do except listen to the radio.

If I stayed home, it was to wash my clothes or do other things that needed to be done. Every chance I got I went out. It didn't matter what I did; it was just important to be out of the house having a good time. Sometimes I went down to the West End to the movies by myself, but mostly I went to dances with my friends.

24 June 1955
Dear Maura,

I wanted to thank you for the picture. It's beautiful, Maura, almost as beautiful as you actually are. I've got all the fellows in the company falling in love with you but I won't give anybody your address.

I found out today that I can take leave up to August 15th. So a friend of mine and I talked about taking a trip to jolly old London sometime during the first week of August. I told him you would probably be able to get him a date with someone. How about it? Let me know if August is okay with you.

Jack and I met at a dance with the band playing the music of the big band era, but I also went to a lot of Irish dances called céilí (pronounced kaylee) dances with my friends. They were like square dances with the upcoming steps announced for the newcomers. There might be just one or two dances the whole evening. They were simple to do and a lot of fun.

```
6 July 1955
Dearest Maura,
    We had a three day weekend this week
because of the 4th of July. But just as I
suspected—it rained for three straight days.
That's the reason why I didn't call. I
couldn't bring myself to go out in the rain.
So we stayed in the billets all weekend,
playing cards and drinking beer. Not ginger
beer either.
    By the way, what does H.O.L.L.A.N.D[3]
mean? I have to give up because I've thought
of every word combination that I know of.
You were right about the meaning of A.W.O.L.
Another thing (I hope you won't be angry)
```

---

[3] Hope our love lasts and never dies.

but I have to show the guys the parts of your letters where you use the word "smashing." They think it's a smashing word and I love you for using it. It reminds me very much of how sweet and charming you are. I hope because I told you, you won't stop saying it. And the rest of what you say is entirely between you and me. Promise!

Before his tour of duty ended, Jack arranged another visit to London in the first week of August. He and Dick flew to London from Germany and my neighbor, Yvonne Field, who was also on holiday, joined us.

12 July 1955

My leave has been definitely approved. It begins on the first of August and I was able to get only seven days. So if we are able to get a flight out right away, we should be able to arrive in London either on the 1st or 2nd of August. Now, when we get there, how should I get in touch with you? Since you'll be on vacation, I won't be able to call you at work, will I? Should I come out to the house? Write and let me know. I don't think we could meet someplace, since I don't know for sure when I get there.

Also, my friend, Dick would be very pleased to date Yvonne. Dick is a very nice guy and I think Yvonne will like him. I hope so.

I've missed you very much since I left. And if I

England

wasn't so much in love with you, I'd never try this crazy thing. But I must see you again before I go home. We have a lot of things to talk over.

Goodnight, Honey—

Yvonne was my best friend during this time; she and I had a lot of fun together. I tried to get Yvonne to come to America with me.

"When you get there, you're probably going to go with him, aren't you?" she asked.

"Probably," I said.

Yvonne and Maura at an office outing in a seashore town

An Irish Face

22 July 1955

Dearest Maura,

Last Saturday night myself and another fellow got caught by the Military Police without a tie on. It's a rule here that when you go out on pass you wear a tie. Well, anyway, the M.P.s turned our name into the Company Commander and he took our civilian clothes away from us for 30 days. But he said I could have them for the time that I'm on leave. So it really isn't so bad.

They're playing *Oh, What a Night It Was* by Johnny Ray on the radio now. I sure wish you were here to listen to it. I'm all by myself down here in the office. We could make some sweet music ourselves. That would be "smashing." Hey what?

I'm hoping we can get a room there at the Douglas House where we stayed before. Then I can make reservations for us some night and we can all go up to the bar and get loaded on good old American whiskey. Maybe not really loaded, just pleasantly drunk. Also, maybe we can sneak into one of those very private clubs we tried before. No matter what we do, as long as you're there I'll have myself a ball.

The four of us spent five days together seeing the sights. We visited the Tower of London, saw the crown jewels, 10 Downing Street, Westminster Abbey, and the

England

changing of the guard at Buckingham Palace. Before Jack left, I promised him I would try to come to America so we could continue seeing each other.

> 8 August 1955
>
> Well, Honey, I'm back to the old dull routine again. We arrived back on Saturday afternoon. I was so tired when I got here I climbed in bed and didn't get up until Monday morning.
>
> We went to the movies tonight. We saw Gone with the Wind. The third time I've seen it. But it was so long ago I didn't remember anything about it.
>
> Darling I want to tell you again how much I enjoyed myself while I was with you. I was never so completely happy for five days before in my life.
>
> Goodnight,
>
> Jack
>
> P.S. I'd give a million pounds for a cup of your coffee right now.

I had told Jack about trying to go to America with my friends using my cousin's birth certificate and what a disaster that had been. This time around I applied for a job with the same agency as before using my own birth certificate.

Jack and I hardly knew each other at this point and I wanted to have a job when I got to America in

An Irish Face

case he decided he didn't like me as much as he thought he did once I got there.

9 August 1955
I just came back from chow and believe it or not they had steak. Not like in the Douglas House but at least it was steak. They keep this up and I might even re-enlist. Ha ha!

One of the guys just brought me in a cold beer. I've got it made now—beer, cigarettes, radio playing nice music, sitting here in my shorts—everything except you.

When Jack left, I contacted the agency that arranged domestic help with families in America. If I obtained a job as a domestic, and worked in America for a year, I would be guaranteed the return fare at the end of the year. I needed to have that security blanket in order to venture across the ocean.

Dick, Jack, and the Government Police Authority, London 1955

England

14 August 1955

Hello Beautiful,

The pictures came back yesterday. I don't know how I'll send them to you. I guess the only way, is to send a few in each letter. I can get them all to you in four or five letters. I think they came out pretty good. Some could have been better if the guy behind the camera knew what he was doing. But anyway you look as beautiful as ever and that's all I care.

This is the fourth letter I've written in one week. For me, this fact alone is amazing. But I have somehow only received one letter. If no one is stealing the mail, then there is only one explanation possible—the letters just aren't being sent out. Is that possible?

Jack

Jack and Maura in London 1955

An Irish Face

I could have had Jack sponsor me to come over without applying for a job, but I wasn't comfortable doing that. I didn't want him to ever think I was only using him to get to America. Jack's letters were very romantic, and he sounded like he was madly in love with me, but he barely knew me and was in love with the idea of me as much as anything.

I needed to have a backup plan in case he decided he wasn't so much in love once I got there. If things didn't work out between us, I planned to work for a year, have an adventure learning about America, and then go back to England.

16 August 1955
Hello Irish,
I'm missing you so damn much I'm going crazy. I can't even keep my mind on my work. If at all possible, honey, try to talk your mother into letting you come as soon as possible. Every day I'm away from you seems like a year. Tell your mother that if she doesn't let you come, I'm coming to London to kidnap you so she might as well give in.

I wrote to Shandon Station in Cork requesting the issue of a reference. I received a letter back saying I needed to furnish not only my place and date of birth, but my parents' names including my mother's maiden name. I also had to list all the different addresses where I resided in Ireland, the period of residence at each address, and the approximate date on which I left Ireland to go to England.

> *16 August 1955*
>
> *My Dearest, Darling, Beautiful, Wonderful Maura,*
>
> *Today in Wurzburg was easier than last week. It took us about one hour to do our work and then we spent the rest of the day listening to records in the Post Store and generally goofing off. Again I got back just in time to quit.*
>
> *How did you make out down to the agency about the papers? Keep working on your end. I wrote my mother and mentioned the wonderful girl I had met in London. So at least she knows you exist. But don't worry about my end; I'll take care of everything when I get home (Only 32 days left, honey.)*
>
> *I miss you so much that if I could see you tomorrow I'd walk to London. Even swim across the channel.*
>
> *Honey, I want you to thank your mother for me for the hospitality I was shown while I was at your house. I enjoyed meeting her very much.*

When I made plans earlier to go to America with my girl friends, it was all just for fun; we were going to see a new country and experience new adventures. This time was different. I was motivated by thoughts of love, marriage, and family. I wanted to be in love with Jack as much as he seemed to be in love with me.

> 19 August 1955
> Dearest Maura,
> I wanted to get this letter out this morning before the mail left but they put me to work before I had a chance to even fully wake up. I'm writing this under the pretense of writing some very important official letter. Well, to me this _is_ the most important letter. What else could it be when I'm writing to the girl that I'm in love with?
> They're after me to go back to work so I'll sign off for now and finish this later. I love you.
> Back again with another typewriter—only it's another day. We got so busy yesterday that I didn't have time to finish this letter.
> You know how good I felt yesterday? Well, this morning I have one of the nicest hangovers anybody could wish to have. I'll never learn. But one good thing came from my drinking. If I hadn't been drinking beer in my room late last night (it was about 12 o'clock) I wouldn't have heard a song requested for me by some girl. I think her name was Maura or something like that. But

England

why she requested *Perfidia*[4] I don't know. Have you ever listened real close to the words in that song? I only hope she didn't mean to have the song tell me something. If you happen to meet this girl ask her what

---

[4] © 1939 Peer International Corp. BMI
To you
My heart cries out "Perfidia"
For I find you, the love of my life
In somebody else's arms

Your eyes are echoing "Perfidia"
Forgetful of the promise of love
You're sharing another's charms

With a sad lament my dreams are faded like a broken melody
While the gods of love look down and laugh
At what romantic fools we mortals be

And now
I find my love was not for you
And so I take it back with a sigh
Perfidia's won
Goodbye

With a sad lament my dreams are faded like a broken melody
While the gods of love look down and laugh
At what romantic fools we mortals be

And now
I find my love was not for you
And so I take it back with a sigh
Perfidia's won
Goodbye
Goodbye

she meant and let me know in your next letter. But for now I'll assume she only requested the song because she knew I liked the song.

   Jack

   P.S. Believe me that song really shook me up.

I continued to write to Jack and make plans to come to America as a domestic employee. Now besides going to dances and movies, I worked on getting all the papers together I needed to make the journey across the ocean.

   23 August 1955

   Last night when you called, the CQ came and told me I had a telephone call. Everybody in the room started yelling about London and somehow I could tell it was you. Then when I got downstairs and picked up the phone, the phone was dead. I asked the CQ where the call came from and he said London. Right then I damn near pulled the phone out of the wall. But all I could do is keep yelling into the phone—with no results. If you want to see a disappointed guy you should have seen me after I knew you were trying to call me and I couldn't talk to you.

   I was especially anxious to talk to you because of that song you requested for me. As I said in my letter I couldn't understand why you requested Perfidia. But

England

today I got a letter and you say they played Flamingo[5] so I guess I got all shook up over nothing. Remember I said we were all sitting around drinking and there was a lot of noise plus just as the announcer said who the song was for the First Sergeant came into the room and we had to get rid of the beer real fast. So I'm sorry about what I said in my last letter. Just forget the last part. Instead just pretend I wrote over and over, "I love you." And I do.

I think I realized a little better how much I do love you these past couple of days. Somehow I began to imagine all kinds of things that could happen that would stop me from ever seeing you again. It got so bad that I actually began to hate—what I hated I don't know but at times I would find myself feeling as if I'd have to smash something. And so much as I dislike admitting it (and I'm probably doing wrong when I do) some of my hatred turned to ~~jeoulo~~ (I don't even know how to spell it.) jealousy.

---

[5] Flamingo (lyrics by Ed Anderson; music by Ted Grouya, 1941)
Flamingo, like a flame in the sky,
Flying over the island to my lover nearby.
[CHORUS]
The wind sings a song to you as you go,
A song that I hear below the murmuring palms.
Flamingo, when the sun meets the sea,
Say farewell to my lover and hasten to me.
Flamingo, in your tropical hue,
Speak of passion undying and a love that is true.
 [CHORUS]

An Irish Face

Well, Maura, that's it. Probably I've expressed myself all wrong and possibly have hurt you. I hope not.

God bless and keep you,

Jack

P.S. How about answering this letter extra fast.

P.S.S. I'm sending some more pictures. This is just about the last one of them—there are about seven or eight prints left. I'll send them in my next letter.

Yvonne, Jack, and Maura, London 1955

I didn't take Jack's fit of jealousy seriously at the time. We were both young and did foolish things. This was just one of those silly things.

England

29 August 1955

Dearest Maura,

Well, honey, about two hours ago I was talking with you and I was feeling wonderful. I even felt as if I might be able to last until I see you again. Now I have that lost and helpless feeling I always have when I think about not seeing you for such a long time. But anyway, thank you very much for calling. It sure helps to know you care enough to want to call.

The typed paper is part of a letter I got from my sister, Bette, the one that stays with my mom. I told you everything was okay on my end. And here is what my mother said:

> Glad you enjoyed your trip—sort of sounds like you have a little case on this Irish lass. I imagine she is as wonderful as you say. Anyway that is only for you to decide. <u>I do wish you could find someone you could be happy with.</u> It is so much better than rambling around.

How's that? We've got it made. But as yet they really don't know anything about us. I just mentioned that I had met a wonderful girl on my first trip to London and that I was going back to see her and that I didn't know what was going to become of it all. I thought it would be better to wait until I get home before I tell them about you coming to the states. It would have been "Max Nix" what they said, but it makes it that much better if

they give their nod of approval. Don't you think so?
   By the way, how are you coming with your mother? How much have you told her? It sure would help too if she approved of your going to the States. Be a good girl so she doesn't get mad. And try to explain it to her. I thought she was so nice when I met her that I don't want us not to be friends.
   In answer to your question about dancing—damn right I'm going to teach you how to dance to Flamingo—although it won't be much of a job after seeing how you can already dance. But that's what I keep thinking about—all these things we can do together when you finally get to L.A.: dancing, swimming, seeing movies, even just sitting home and talking. It's going to be wonderful being with you again.

Mother and I were so ignorant of the law; we didn't realize that even though I had never been formally adopted, Mother was my legal guardian. I could furnish her information and she could sign the papers as my guardian. We thought I needed to provide information about my "natural" mother [that is how she is referred to in Ireland] so I wrote to Sacred Heart Hospital and requested details about her and asked them to provide me with my birth certificate.

England

Jack and Dick in London, 1955
"Not a care in the world"

1 Sept 1955
Hello Beautiful,

A funny thing happened today with the mail. Along with your last letter I received one postmarked the 19th of August. It was the letter where you told me you were going to the States for sure. So you see until now I didn't know that the agency had told you that you definitely could go. It also told me for the first time your mother had approved of your going. I don't know what could have happened to the letter for so long, but it was nice hearing these things. Hurry to me as fast as you can, Darling. I miss you so very much.

I went to Darmstadt again today and did a lot of nothing. I'm getting so I like these trips out of town. It gives me a chance to relax and day dream about you. It's also nice to come back and have some mail from the woman I love waiting for me. Keep the letters coming, honey, as fast as you can write.

    Good night, Darling

    Jack

    P.S. The money isn't much but I thought it would help with the phone call. This is also the last of the pictures. I love you.

Maura and Yvonne, lunch in the park, London 1955

When the letter arrived from Sacred Heart in response to my request, I sat down at the kitchen table to read it. I was just home from work, and Mother was cooking dinner. The Reverend Mother wrote:

```
According to our books your mother
and yourself were discharged from
Bessboro' on 1st April, 1935, and
there is no record of your being
adopted, of course adoption was not
```

England

legal in Ireland at that time. We have never heard from your mother since then. If you require your Birth Certificate, write to the Registrar, Board Room, Douglas Road, Cork.

6 September 1955

I got your letter with the answers to my questions. If I had told you exactly what I wanted you to say I couldn't have written a nicer letter. But one thing Maura, I don't want you to worry about—that's my meeting another girl and liking her more than you. How could I fall for somebody else when I love the most perfect girl in the world already? If I don't hold you in my arms soon, I'll lose my head and do something desperate. So get those people at the agency on the ball and tell them to stop keeping two people apart.

I heard on the radio that the temperature in Southern California has been over 100 degrees. Sure hope it keeps up while I'm home so I'll be able to get some time in at the beaches. Then when you come, we can spend a lot of time there together. Just the two of us on a blanket with a portable radio. Man, that sounds like the greatest to me. Then nights we can go dancing, or to the movies, or just stay home and watch TV with the lights out. Smashing!

An Irish Face

Reading the Reverend Mother's letter triggered all the sadness I'd tucked inside me for the last 20 years and plunged me into a fit of weeping like I'd never experienced before. I sobbed and wailed uncontrollably. A part of me watched in wonder as these harsh guttural sounds came out of me, and there was nothing I could do to stop it. I didn't know I could cry like this.

Sykes'Regulars
LET'S GO!
HQ & HQ CO. 20th INFANTRY REGIMENT
[not dated]

Hello Darling,

All kinds of things have happened since I left Germany. We left on schedule and everything went smooth for the first three days on the ship and then we hit some rough weather. About half of the fellows started to get seasick and the other half was merely waiting their turn (including myself.) But this was nothing. After a couple more days we ran into a real honest to goodness hurricane. After three days of this we finally hit some good weather and steamed on into New York. But the storm had slowed us down so that it took us two extra days.

After we hit New York the fellows going to California had a big disappointment. Up until then, we thought the Army would fly us across country. But they had buses waiting to take us to trains and so we headed out for California aboard a train. Four days later we arrived at Fort Ord, California—that's where we are to get discharged. The date was the 1st day of October.

But then my luck changed. About five minutes after I arrived at Fort Ord my sister and brother-in-law came after me. My brother-in-law is a Captain stationed at Fort Ord so he was able to get me a pass and I went home with them.

I didn't know anyone could cry like this. My display of raw emotion must have frightened Mother but she did nothing to comfort me. All she could do was tell me over and over again, "It's not my fault."

18 October 1955

Today I got your letter with the contracts. I was terribly sorry when I learned that you must come to Hartford, Connecticut and the job doesn't pay a hell of a lot. But I guess we are stuck. The worst thing about the deal is the part about having to stay 12 months. But I want to know if it would be possible for us to pay off the $250 before the time is up so you could leave. Find out and tell me in your next letter.

I'm a little worried about you being by yourself in Hartford until I get there. What if one of those Connecticut fellows fall as much in love with the redhead from London as I am? Nobody will ever love you more than I do, but he *might make you believe it. So be good and watch out for all the damn Americans until I get there.*

The family is anxious to meet you and from your pictures they can understand why I'm anxious to have them meet you.

They're showing pictures of Peter Townsend on television. [6]

Finally, exhausted and physically spent from crying so hard, I felt a peace come over me. My life had begun differently than I would have wished, but there was nothing I could do to change it. I could, however, do something about my future.

30 October 1955
Hello Darling,

By the time you arrive in the States I hope to have saved enough money to make the trip east and pay the people the fare for your trip. Then you'll be able to make the trip back to Compton with us right away. I say "us" because my mother will be coming east with me. She

---

[6] Group Captain Townsend is best known for his ill-fated romance with Princess Margaret. Despite his distinguished career, as a divorced man there was no chance of marriage with the princess and their relationship caused enormous controversy in the mid 1950s.

http://en.wikipedia.org/wiki/Peter_Townsend_(RAF_officer)

England

wants to see all her old friends plus I still have a sister living in Pennsylvania (that's the state right next to New York.)

If the people won't let you go then Mom will return by herself and I'll get a job in Stamford myself. I hope it doesn't seem to you that I'm telling you what you have to do but it's only my idea how we might be able to handle everything. We can talk it all over when you get here and decide what we think would be best.

Tonight is Halloween night. I don't know if they have anything like it in England. It's a combination of a lot of customs. It's supposed to be the night that all the ghosts roam around, so everybody gets dressed up in costume and all the kids go around knocking on house doors and the people give them candy. We've had at least 200 kids knock on our door tonight and I've been trying to watch television, but can't so I gave up and just stood at the door and gave out candy. My three nieces and nephews went out and came back with three great big sacks full of the stuff.

I'm working now. Doing something I never did before—drafting. It's real complicated and I don't know anything about it but at least I get a paycheck every week. I get about $65 a week or about 25 pounds. That probably seems like a lot of money in England but here it doesn't last very long.

An Irish Face

I wrote to the Registrar in Cork as the Reverend Mother had directed and obtained my birth certificate. I discovered my first mother had named me Mary O'Sullivan after her, and she was a maid by occupation. There was a line drawn through the space where the information about my father belonged. Whoever he was, he didn't want to acknowledge his part in my existence.

At this point in my life, it didn't matter. There was a handsome young man in California who was crazy about me and couldn't wait for me to come to America. I was ready to go.

10 November 55

How's my wonderful Irish lass tonight? I hope you are packing your bags right this minute for the big trip. Every night I say a little prayer that it will be real soon. I miss you so much. Sometimes it gets so bad I think I might bust.

I have everything planned for the trip east. Last week I put the first $30 away for your payment of the fare. So by the time you arrive I'll be able to come to you right away.

After getting a medical examination and arranging a visa appointment with the American Consulate, I received a letter from the Overseas

England

Domestic Service and a cheque in the amount of £6.0.4d [six pounds, four pence] to cover the cost of my visa fee and the agency's fee. I also had a copy of the application submitted by my new employers in Stamford, Connecticut.

> *13 November 1955*
>
> *Tonight on television they had a woman comedian from London and as all the family watched the show I would have given a million dollars if you could have been with us. Please write and tell me about when you'll be able to come. I'm getting more money than I figured on at my job so I'll be able to save your fare sooner.*
>
> *If for some reason you decided not to come or if it was impossible for you to come, all the things I'm working for now, and all my dreams of our happiness would be wasted. Please let me hear you tell me in a letter that you will come no matter what.*

```
    21 November 1955
When are you finally going to get your
papers to come? Remember we were talking
about you being here for Thanksgiving?
Thursday is the day and no sign of Maura.
And I don't go for the idea of waiting until
St. Patrick's Day like you mentioned.
    Sure do wish you could have made it for
Thanksgiving though, Honey. It's a big day
in the Brown family. As many as possible of
```

the big clan get together and have a big feast. One thing is nice about the whole deal—I get the day off from work and still get paid for it.

I thought you might be interested in the things I cut out of one of our magazines the other day. I'm not sending them to ruin your idea of Johnny Ray because I know how much you like his singing but I thought maybe you would get a kick out of knowing about it.[7]

1 December 1955

I got your letter today and damn near had a heart attack. The first thing I saw when I opened the letter was the bit in the form from the Embassy where they tell you not to plan transportation. Before I could read anymore I had already called the American Embassy every choice name I've ever heard. But after I read the whole thing I think it sounds very promising.

To explain Thanksgiving would take hours, honey, but I'll try to give you an idea. After the pilgrims had landed in America way back about 1640, they decided that they should give thanks to God for the privilege of living in such a wonderful place and for having so much success with their harvest. So they set aside one day for a

---

[7] The magazine article is missing but information about the singer is available on Wikipedia including two arrests for soliciting sex from men and his long term relationship with his manager, Bill Franklin.

England

big feast after they had harvested all the crops, and to give thanks—and so Thanksgiving Day. The way it is celebrated now is still about the same. The big part of the day is the Thanksgiving turkey dinner. It is also proper to thank God for all the things he has given you during the year. This year I thanked Him for bringing you into my life and asked Him if he couldn't hurry and bring you to me again. That's my one prayer right now.

    I heard that London was covered with a big "smog" last week. Was it very bad? L.A. (you did very good in your last letter) has quite a lot of smog too but the sunshine makes up for it. It rained here today—for the second time since I've been here.

    How come you always say just "God Bless?" Is that how you say it in England? Also, why do your letters smell so wonderful? Whatever it is, keep it up!!

19 December 1955

If my writing is a little sloppy tonight, Honey, it's because I'm being helped by my little niece, Cherie. She's sitting next to me and keeps knocking into my arm. She just asked me if she could write something, so she'll say hello at the end of this.

    Well, Darling, Christmas is almost here. We have our tree up now and we put the first presents under it today. If only you could be here with us, Irish, it's the only present I would want. But soon, Honey, soon. I spoke to the boss today about taking off from work for my trip east. He's trying to get me a "leave of absence" so I can go back to work when we get back.

Maura, I'm sending you the money for the phone call. I want you to wait until you get the word from your final interview and then call me and make me either the happiest or the saddest man in the world. Find out when it will be Sunday, January 8th here in California and then call me anytime on that day. And don't forget about the difference in our time. I think there is either eight or nine hours difference but which way I don't know. Also make sure you find out for California and not New York because there is a difference between them too.

Goodnight
Jack.

Hello Maura,
Hurry and come to us.
We all miss you.
Cherie

28 December 1955
Hello Irish,
By the time you receive this you should know whether you have the visa or not. The thing I'm waiting for now is your telephone call. I forgot to tell you the number though—it's NE 12409. You'll be able to get the number by just asking for an L.A.

```
operator. The way I would like it to work is
for me to pay back the money for your fare
right away and ask the people if you can
leave.
     I got your Christmas present. It was
beautiful and I've worn it already. Thank
you very much. Now I can say I have a real
imported tie.
     The way things stand now it will be
about the middle of February before I can
come to get you. It will be until then
before I can save enough money to make the
trip east and also have the money ready to
pay for your fare. All together it will take
about $750.00 or that's about 270 pounds.
Once we get this taken care of we'll be
together. And that is worth all the money in
the world.
```

The agency reserved accommodations for me on the R.M.S. Queen Mary scheduled to sail from Southampton on 12 January, 1956. Though I would still always be Maura to my family and friends, I was off to a new land with a new name, the name I was given at birth—Mary O'Sullivan.

Part Three

America

Say what you mean, mean what you say, but don't say it mean.

Author Unknown

An Irish Face

Cunard R.M.S. Queen Mary

America

ABSTRACT OF THE LOG OF THE CUNARD STEAM-SHIP COMPANY LIMITED
R.M.S. "QUEEN MARY"
CAPTAIN D. W. SORRELL

SOUTHAMPTON AND CHERBOURG TO NEW YORK

Date (1956)	Dist.	Latitude N.	Longitude W.	Weather, etc.
Thurs. Jan, 12				At 10.01 (G.M.T.) left Ocean Terminal, So'ton
,, ,, ,,				At 12.27 (G.M.T.) NAB Tower abeam
,, ,, ,,				At 16.12 (F.T.) arrived Cherbourg
,, ,, ,,				At 19.57 (F.T.) left Cherbourg
Friday ,, 13	509	49.53	14.41	Strong breeze rough sea, mod. swell, o'cast, clear
Saturday ,, 14	730	47.54	32.58	Strong gale, rough sea and very heavy swell
Sunday ,, 15	719	43.23	48.58	Fresh gale, rough sea and heavy swell
Monday ,, 16	711	41.27	64.41	Mod. breeze, mod. sea and swell, c'ldy and clear
Tuesday ,, 17	422	to Ambrose	Chan. L.V.	At 04.25 (E.S.T.) Ambrose Channel L.V. abeam. Arrival
Total	3,091	nautical miles		

PASSAGE—4 days, 14 hours, 28 minutes   AVERAGE SPEED—27.98 knots

An Irish Face

R.M.S. "QUEEN MARY" Monday, January 16, 1956

. Farewell Dinner .

V.8 Juice

Mixed Fruit Cocktail

Hors d'Œuvre:
Salade Russe   Pâté de Foie sur Croûte   Cod Roes, Ravigote
Sardines in Oil   Asperges, Vinaigrette   Céleris, Mignonnette

Consommé Souveraine   Velouté Reine Margot

Poached Halibut, Vin Blanc
Fried Fillet of Sole, Rémoulade Sauce

Rizotto, Valencienne

Vol-au-Vent, Régence

Baked American Ham, Madère

Roast Turkey, Farcie, Cranberry Sauce

GRILL (to order): Vienna Steak, Mushroom Sauce

Green Peas   Corn on the Cob

Boiled and Roast Potatoes

COLD: Roast Ribs and Sirloin of Beef, Horseradish Cream
Roast Veal

Salads: Lettuce   Tossed Green   Jack O'Lantern
Mayonnaise and Russian Dressings

Montmorency Pudding, Cherry Sauce

Assorted Pastries

Ice Cream: Vanilla   Peach
Fresh Fruit

Coffee

Passengers on Special Diet are especially invited to make known their requirements to the Chief Tourist Steward
Speciality Foods for Infants are available on request

America

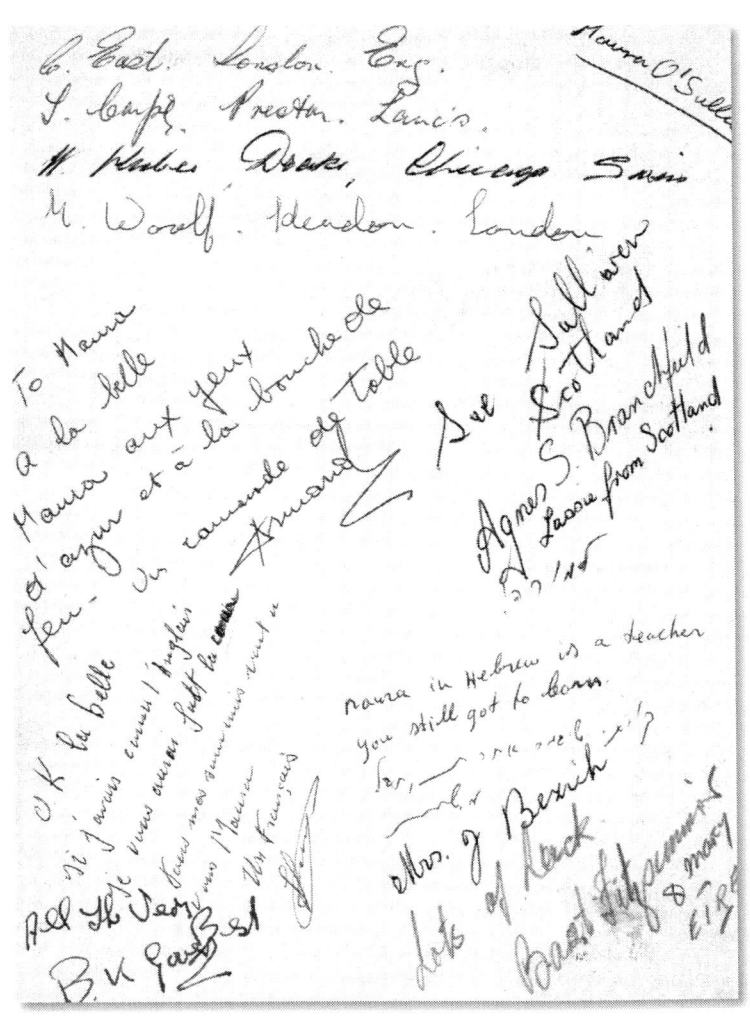

Farewells on the Queen Mary

An Irish Face

Thursday, 12 January 1956, at 10 o'clock in the morning, I set sail from Southampton to New York Harbor on the Queen Mary. We arrived in New York on the morning of Tuesday, January 17th before dawn. All of us on the ship were disappointed as it was too dark to see the Statue of Liberty.

America

Dinner on the Queen Mary was a feast every night. We could choose between Pâté de Foie sur Croûte or Asperges Vinaigrette. There was also poached halibut, American ham, tenderloin steak, roast turkey, rolled ox tongue, roast ribs, and sirloin of beef with horseradish cream served cold. For dessert we had our fill of puddings, pastries, and ice cream.

On the voyage from England I ate corn on the cob for the first time but didn't have a taste for it—too stringy. That same year, Jack and I went to a beach party with some friends, and I again ate corn on the cob. I also drank too much and got sick. I blamed it on the corn.

An older woman shared a cabin with me on the ride over the Atlantic. She was in her forties and was going to America to visit her children. She took the bottom bunk, and I took the top one. There was a hat-making contest on the ship, and I was quite impressed with the hat she styled out of paper.

Two girls from Scotland were going to New Rochelle to work as domestic servants, and we became friends on the ship, but we didn't stay in touch once we landed. The trip lasted four and a half days and with more guys than girls on board, every night was a party. It was the end of the big band era, and we danced to Frank Sinatra, Dean Martin, and other crooners. I became friends with many of the passengers on the ship, and we spent our farewell dinner on January 16th signing each other's menus.

BEFORE LEAVING ENGLAND I signed an agreement that I would work for the K. family for one year. Mr. and Mrs. K. hired me to do the domestic work on the second floor of their home, and I was expected to keep my uniforms, my room, and myself neat and clean. I did the laundry except for the sheets and shirts which were sent out to the cleaners, and helped take care of their two younger children, a boy and girl ages four and five. For my work, I received $100 a month plus room and board. Because Mr. K. paid the $250 passage fee to America, my monthly sum was to be reduced for six months until it was paid off. If I stayed the full year, I would receive a bonus equal to the return fare.

Mr. K. met me at the harbor in New York, and we took the train to Connecticut. From the train we took a taxi to their family home.

25 January 1956
My darling, Maura,
After reading your letter and realizing how you must feel being alone in a strange place and having a job like you have, every day that you have to stay there is torture to me. I guess I couldn't blame you if you just

turned around and went back. But, please believe me, Maura, that I have just one goal in my life—and that is to be with you as soon as possible and then to try to make you as happy as I possibly can.

Now about my trip east. We will be leaving California on the 11th of February. I figure it will take about five days to cross country and then about two days for me to get up to Connecticut. So you see it won't be long before I'll be knocking on the door. And then we'll see whether or not you can come with me. I think I'll have to kidnap you.

Tell me, how come you're using O'Sullivan now? Is that your name on your birth certificate or what? I sure was surprised to get a letter from Miss M. O'Sullivan. I think she must be a wonderful girl.

My work day began at 7:45 in the morning with breakfast. I worked through the day (with a rest period of two hours in the afternoon) until the end of the 7 o'clock dinner. On Thursdays after breakfast and every other Sunday, I was free to do what I wanted.

The K. family owned a five-and-ten-cent store, and their marriage was the second for both of them. They appeared to be an unhappy couple. They fought through most dinners— often about money.

Mrs. K. was much younger than Mr. K.; she in her late thirties to early forties. Mr. K.'s children from his first marriage were older, and I didn't know anything about them. Mrs. K. had a 14-year-old daughter living at home, and the two little ones in my care were from their marriage to each other.

I remember once when the teenage daughter was going to a dance, a local store brought dresses out to the house for her to try on. Another memory is of a time when she got mad at me (I can't remember why), and to get even with me she put all of her clean clothes in the laundry to create more work for me. For the most part though, we got along fine.

The two little children ate dinner by themselves at their own small table, and I sat with them. Sometimes they didn't want to eat their dinner, but they really didn't give me much trouble. I took my meals in the kitchen with the other maid, Roxie, and we got along great. My room was in the back of the house on the main floor, and I shared a bath with the children. Roxie (who was black) had a room on the same floor but had her own bath.

ROXIE TOOK CARE of the downstairs rooms and did the cooking for the family. She treated me well, and I enjoyed spending time with her. Once she took me to her daughter's house to meet her family on our day off. I bought a cake and had their names put on it, but I got them wrong. The older daughter was

America

upset about it, but they all liked me anyway. Roxie set me up on a date once with a young white man that she knew, but I wasn't interested in him. Jack was making plans for me to come to California.

WHILE JACK WAS in the service, his mother and some of his siblings moved from New York to California. I had no idea how far apart these two states were until I accepted the domestic job in Connecticut. In England or Ireland you could drive across the country in a day.

Jack was working for North American Aviation, and he arranged a formal leave of absence to attend to personal business in the state of New York. With his company's approval, he set off across country with his mother, to bring me back to California with them.

30 January 1955

Well, Irish, one of us goofed yesterday. I must have misunderstood you when you said you had no place to go. I thought it might be nicer to talk to you in the evening than during the day. Of course it was still afternoon here when I called. But the woman at the house told me she didn't know whether you'd be back before the next morning or not. So I take it you did find some place to go with someone?

An Irish Face

England was so much like Ireland, I never felt lonesome when I lived there. For the most part America felt like a completely different world to me but sitting in church on a Sunday morning in Connecticut, it struck me how much it was like the one in Cork. I became so overwhelmed with homesickness, it made me cry.

I GOT ALONG FINE with Mrs. K., but Mr. K. was a mess. He started drinking in the morning as soon as he got up, and he walked around with just a robe on—tying and untying the belt—exposing himself to whoever was there. At midday, Mr. K showered, dressed, and took his wife to lunch at the country club.

Every Sunday morning, Roxie prepared breakfast for Mr. and Mrs. K. and I took it to them in their bedroom.

One time I entered the room with their tray and Mr. K. was lying next to his wife with his aroused genitals completely exposed. Neither one of them said anything.

I was so ignorant at the time, but now I realize that even though Mrs. K. was educated, she felt as powerless as I did to stop her husband's vulgar behavior.

America

7 February 1956

I love you

My Darling Maura,
    I love you, Irish, and I always will.
    We leave in just three days, honey. I wish I was there now so that I could apologize for the way I felt and take back all the things I said in my last letter. I should have realized how you must have felt on your day off just sitting around. Well, anyway, I understand why you weren't there when ~~you~~ I called, and I'll prove it in just a few days.
    The best thing I've heard in a long time is when you wrote in your letter that you'd

An Irish Face

be all ready to go when I get there. I've been talking to some immigration people and they tell me that there is no way that they should be able to hold you there.

I watched Bob Hope's TV program tonight. He was broadcasting from London and they showed shots of the city and I recognized some of them but you could probably have named them all. I even forget the name of the theatre now, but it wasn't the Palladium. I recognized Talfalger Square (is that right?) and it sure brought back some wonderful memories.

America

Last Friday night I was missing you extra special, so I got out all the pictures and tried to relive all the moments I was with you. Do you remember our picnic in the park? We never did finish our hamburgers. I guess we just forgot about them. Beautiful, did you know I loved you very, very much. Well, I do. I'll also prove this in a few days. Believe Me!!!

Bedtime right now, honey, so I'll say goodnight and God Bless you and keep you for me.
 I love you,
XXXXXXXXXXX Jack

(Final letter Jack wrote to Maura before arriving in Connecticut)

Jack and his mother stopped in Shinglehouse, Pennsylvania to visit Jack's sister, Madalyn, who married at the age of 16 and still lived there with her family. After one night at his sister's house, Jack drove to Connecticut to get me.

When Jack arrived, I'd been with the K. family for a little over a month. They were planning a vacation to the Virgin Islands and were expecting me to come with them to help with the younger children.

I felt like such a criminal. I couldn't even tell Roxie that I was planning to go with Jack to California. Before telling Mr. and Mrs. K. that I was quitting, Jack and I visited the immigration office in New York City. They confirmed that with my resident alien green card, I could stay in America legally even if I no longer worked for the K. family. I needed a sponsor in America who was willing to accept all "known or unknown liabilities of the said Mary O'Sullivan." On the 27th day of February, 1956, Muriel Brown, my future mother-in-law swore that she would do so.

MR. K. WAS VERY ANGRY when I told him I was going to California with Jack and his mother. I'd signed a one-year contract with him and he expected me to honor it. He threatened to have me deported if I tried to leave with Jack. He also complained to the Overseas Domestic Service of London about me. Before leaving Connecticut, I received a letter from Millard A. Ring, the attorney for the Overseas Domestic Service stating Mr. K.'s intention of taking legal action against me, not only for the monies he paid for my passage, but for other damages resulting from the breach of my contract. In the letter, Mr. Ring also scolded me for leaving Mr. K.:

> In this connection, I must further caution you against any action on your part whereby you would leave Mr. K., who is personally responsible for you, and depart in the company of a man to whom you are not married. This would be a most serious mistake on your part.

JACK OFFERED MR. K. $175.00 to cover the unpaid portion of my passage and Jack's mother signed an affidavit stating she accepted responsibility for me and relieved Mr. K. of any obligations they had toward me. Finally, on February 29, Mr. K accepted Jack's money and signed a receipt stating that the money received was full payment of all obligations and that I was free to seek other employment.

As much as I was glad to be free of the K. family, I felt guilty about breaking the contract I had with them. For years I was so ashamed of myself that I didn't talk about it. I knew when I signed the document, there was only a slim possibility I would stay for a year. In his letters to me, Jack made it clear he would not wait that long for us to be together.

Roxie wasn't happy about my decision to leave. "Are you sure you want to go off with him? The leather in his car is all torn. He can't be worth much money," she told me. I wasn't worried about that. I packed my bags, and Jack and I drove off in the Oldsmobile his mother gave him when he got out of the army. We stopped in Pennsylvania at his sister's house to pick up Jack's mother, and from there we headed to California sitting on leather seats with the loose stitching that worried Roxie. Jack drove both ways since his mother had quit driving when she moved to California, and I hadn't yet learned to drive.

THE FOUR DAY TRIP from Connecticut to California was an exciting, romantic adventure for me. I was fascinated with the vastness and beauty of the countryside. Going through Texas, we ran into a sandstorm so dense my white blouse turned brown. All across America, the women looked younger and dressed more stylish than the women I knew in Ireland and England. They also carried themselves differently. When I visited with other women who were raised in Europe, they told me they noticed it too. Things just seemed brighter in America: the houses, cars, clothes, the people themselves. Wherever we went, the image I had of America from watching American-made movies as a young girl came to life.

AFTER WE ARRIVED in California, my future sister-in-law Bette got me a job at the manufacturing plant where she worked as a bookkeeper. The company made trophies, medals, and pins and I worked on the assembly line.

On May 4th, 1956, Jack and I, his brother, George and George's girlfriend, Bernadine (Bunny) left after work and drove to Las Vegas. We arrived early in the morning, got a room, and took a nap.

Las Vegas was amazing. The whole weekend was one endless day. Everything stayed open 24 hours, and when you were in the casinos you didn't know if it was day or night. When we woke up from the nap, we got a license at the court house and then went shopping and bought dresses for our weddings. I purchased a soft beige-pink satin dress with three-quarter sleeves and a rounded collar. I also bought a sleeveless shift, white with black polka dots, which fell just below the knee and a jacket with short cuffed sleeves in black with white polka dots. I can't remember what Bunny wore, but she was always a smart dresser, and we both looked quite stylish in our new outfits.

We found a place that would marry us, and just before midnight on May 5, 1956 we were married in a double ceremony. Everyone was a little high. Bunny and I couldn't stop giggling throughout the ceremony. When the judge asked me to say Jack's name I couldn't remember it; Jack had to help me.

We also went to a show that weekend. I was a big fan of Johnny Ray's *Little White Clouds That Cry*. I had seen him once in London and was very excited to see him again. When he made the same mistakes that were so funny in the London show, I realized it was just part of the act and it put me off him forever.

THE YEAR 1956 was an eventful one for me. I sailed on the Queen Mary to America, breached a contract with the family who made it possible for me to come, traveled from Connecticut to California with my future husband, got another job, married, bought a house with Jack, and became pregnant with my first child.

Alanna was born in April 1957; Zana followed the next year; Michelle the following year, and two years after that, in 1961, Lisa arrived. Both Michelle and Lisa were delivered cesarean.

I stopped working in the factory when Alanna was born and stayed home to care for the children. We lived in a brand-new house in a neighborhood in

America

Whittier, a nice town just a few miles southeast of Los Angles. Jack's sister, Bette lived down the street with her family. Our house had four bedrooms, and Jack's mother, Muriel, lived with us and babysat Bette's children. Muriel had her own bedroom and bathroom.

My mother-in-law was good to me, and I never minded her living with us, but she died when I was pregnant with Michelle. The other young women in the neighborhood liked Muriel too. We had a great time playing Canasta. Many women in the neighborhood were Jewish, and it was my first exposure to the Jewish faith.

Jack and I did fine until after Lisa was born. He was gifted at math and worked as a draftsman before he was promoted to hydraulic sales. He was very ambitious and worked hard. After his promotion, he began drinking with the guys at the company. He came home drunk most Friday nights. I got mad at him, but when I complained, he used my lack of education as a weapon against me to a very good effect. He said it was his right to have a drink with friends, and it was my foolish thinking that was the problem.

As a young girl, when Mother referred to me as "a fine girl," I felt like such a big ugly thing. Jack knew how to make me feel the same way. I never understood how someone could get pleasure out of hurting other people, but that was all Jack seemed to know at times.

It was as though demons came up inside of him, and he couldn't stop himself, or rather he didn't stop himself.

A COUPLE OF TIMES in the early years of our marriage I was so mad at Jack, I kicked him out of the house. Sometimes he left of his own volition with the expectation I would run after him—which I never did. One of the times Jack left was in 1972. I remember we experienced an earthquake while he was gone. The girls were in grade school and junior high at the time. I was still so unsure of my language skills, I was taking a class for people whose English was a second language. I think the reason Jack left then (I don't know for sure) was so I would have to quit school and look for work.

OUR FIGHTING scared the children. Once, after Jack left, Michelle asked me, "Are we going to be poor?" She had a friend whose parents were divorced, and her friend's mother struggled terribly to keep food on the table and her daughter properly clothed. I was as terrified as Michelle of having to live that way. "Of course not," I told her.

Jack had some horrible moments, but he wasn't a horrible man. Sometimes he could be a lot of fun, and he helped me with the children. Compared to the men in Ireland that I'd known, he was a great help. He changed diapers, helped bathe the girls, and fed them their bottles. He played games with them and would act silly to get us all laughing.

He always complimented the dinner I prepared in a most genuine way, and he was very demonstrative. He taught the children and me to be comfortable with hugs and kisses. And he was not afraid to tell his daughters that he loved them. He told them often, "On a scale of ten, I love you a ten."

Back row: Michelle, Maura, Jack, Lisa,
Front row: Zana and Alanna

An Irish Face

I HAD NOT GROWN up with displays of affection, and apparently many of the neighbors hadn't either. Some of them commented on the fact that our girls would stop playing and run to kiss their dad when he got home from work.

When the children were young, we spent a lot of weekends camping, boating, and water skiing with the girls and their friends. We'd start in May and go through to September. It was a fun time for all of us.

We had many good times as a family, and I wished there were more, but sometimes Jack would turn on us and say ugly things. It made the girls tense not knowing when their dad would explode. I thought if I tried harder I could make it better; it was what kept me going.

I began to wonder what was wrong with me. I loved my children dearly, and we lived in a beautiful home. Why wasn't I satisfied? What was wrong with me? Mother had spent her life striving for money as a means to happiness. If money really could buy happiness, I should be ecstatic since I had material possessions she could only dream of having when I was a child.

The truth was it didn't matter how much money we had. If Jack didn't treat me and the children right, I was never going to be happy with him. At the same time, I didn't want to live in a house again where the cupboards were bare.

One day I sat down and thought about all of the problems I had with Jack and what life would be like if I left him. At the end of the day, I came to the conclusion even though my life was far from perfect, I would stay with Jack and make the best of it for the girls and me. There was no way I could provide for them as well as Jack could if we stayed married. I wanted more for my children than what my mother was able to give me. I also knew I didn't want a man other than Jack helping me raise our daughters. By staying with Jack, our girls would be better off financially than if I divorced him. It was as simple and as complicated as that.

MANY PEOPLE CONSIDER watching television a waste of time, but for me, it opened a window that allowed me to view the world in a different way than I had before. The family in Connecticut had a television as well as Jack's family, and I spent hours watching whatever program was on at the time.

During the 60s and 70s when people of color and women demanded their equal rights, it had a profound impact on me. No matter what race or ethnic background we came from, humans aren't all that different from one another. We are all searching for the same thing; we just go about it in different ways.

An Irish Face

Discovering this allowed me to accept my deficits and shed the misinformation I'd learned in my childhood about other people who looked and lived differently than our family did. Other people had as much right to be on the planet as I did, and just because they were different, wasn't a reason to be afraid of them.

It wasn't just the people on television that I saw differently. I could see qualities in my friends and acquaintances that made it possible for me to connect with them, regardless of their looks, money, or level of education. My new found view of the world made it possible for me to deal with the pain I experienced from not knowing my biological mother, and it gave me the courage to pursue knowledge in other areas of my life.

WHEN MOTHER CAME to visit me in California in the mid-sixties, she gave me a string of pearls she'd purchased in a pub. In England, the pubs were gathering places where folks came to drink, talk, and occasionally buy and sell things. Mother assured me the pearls were real. I thought they were beautiful, and I told her so, but I wasn't sure they were genuine because I didn't trust she always told me the truth. As a child, I had experienced her lying to other people so many times. Not only did she tell deliberate lies, she often made me tell the same lies. Even so, I hoped the pearls were real as it was the nicest gift she had ever given me.

I didn't find out the truth until years later when Michelle told me she was considering buying a pearl necklace since her birthstone was pearl. I wanted her to save her money for college so I offered to have my pearls restrung for her. In the car on the way to the jewelry story, I hoped and prayed the pearls were worth the expense of restringing. No one else knew how worried I was. At the jewelry store, we learned you can put your teeth on the pearls and bite gently. If they feel gravelly on your teeth they are the real thing but if they feel smooth, they are imitation. I was immensely relieved to discover my mother had given me genuine pearls.

After her visit to California, ten years went by before I saw Mother again. In 1974, I had a job making cosmetics. My sister Annie called from London to tell me Mother was ill and wanted me to come for a visit. Jack said of course I could go. By then, I suspected all of his motives, and I thought he only wanted to impress on my family what a good guy he was.

It had been quite a while since I'd spent time with my mother and sisters, and when I arrived in London, I was struck by how much Mother and Annie looked alike. When I casually mentioned it to Mother, she got very angry. Her reaction surprised me, and I wanted to shock some sense into her. I told her she sounded like she hated Annie. I was the one who ended up shocked. "I do hate her," she told me.

We spent the evening drinking in a London pub and then went back to Annie's flat and continued the party. As we drank beer and laughed and talked about old times, Annie said to me, "You are different from us. You come from good stock. Your father was a doctor." (Delia, Kittie's daughter, on a later visit told me she'd heard it was the doctor's son who got my mother pregnant.) This was all new information to me as well as the fact that Mother shared a bus ride with the woman who gave birth to me. When Mother took me as a baby from the convent back to Cork City, my first mother was also on that bus. Mother described her to me as "a cold and distant woman who didn't say much."

All this talk about my origins made both Angela and me curious about our natural mothers. Mother was well enough that we didn't need to stay with her for my entire visit so Angela, Mary (Annie's youngest daughter), and I went to Ireland to visit Sacred Heart where Angela and I were born.

The nun we spoke to at the convent gave us a grand tour of the place but told us nothing about our history, and there was no way we were going to get

America

any information out of her. You just know with some people you talk to, they are not going to tell you anything they don't want to tell you. She informed us the nuns didn't stay in contact with the girls after they gave birth and left the convent. She also told us it was best not to look for our mothers because we were our mothers' secret and it would not be a good idea to disrupt their lives by showing up after all this time.

This nun was quite proud of how the convent took care of the girls and their secrets. They routed the girls' letters through London and America so the people in their home towns would think the girls were off seeing the world rather than working in a convent waiting to give birth.

On our tour of the convent we saw some of these young girls playing cards together while on break. There were a lot of young pregnant women doing chores around the place, hauling buckets of stuff, earning their keep. And there were babies sleeping in the nursery. Babies who had no idea they were destined to be sent away from their mothers to new homes picked by the nuns just as Angela and I had been sent to live with Mother.

TWENTY YEARS LATER, in 1995, I visited Ireland again with my daughter Lisa. She and I planned to visit Sacred Heart so she could see where I was born. As we drove up the driveway of the convent, I felt a pain in my throat so severe I told Lisa to stop the car. I could not make myself go there again. After we turned around and left, the pain subsided but my throat remained sore for sometime afterward.

I FELT ABANDONED by my first mother, but I never blamed her. I knew what the conditions were. If a girl got pregnant and didn't marry for whatever reason, she had two choices: she could raise her child under a blanket of shame and poverty, or she could relinquish her child.

My childhood may have been worse than some people had to endure, but it was much better than others. There was a family next door to us who fostered two kids for awhile but then sent one back. I was glad Mother was never so disappointed in me that she sent me back. At the same time I secretly longed for my natural mother to come for me.

What gave me the most pain from my childhood was my lack of formal education. When my daughters reached school age, I determined they were going to like school. I didn't want them to miss a minute of the school day unless they were really and truly sick. At the beginning of each year, I got the girls all new school clothes including new underwear and socks. They also got new crayons and notebooks.

Jack was always complaining about how I spent *his* money. Every school year we fought about the new clothes and supplies until finally I grew weary of it and told him, "Fine. You do the shopping if you think I do such a poor job. I'm turning it all over to you." He never bothered me about it again, and I continued to do the shopping with the girls.

I realize now, I should have confronted Jack more often. As a child I'd learned to survive in difficult times by blending into the woodwork as best I could. The idea of confronting my mother was unthinkable. What if she threw me out? Where would I go? Confronting Jack felt like confronting Mother. There was too much at stake, and it took too much energy to stand up to him. By the time I was strong enough to say, "Enough is enough"—it was too late. I had bottled up so much anger toward him over the years; I no longer wanted the marriage.

WHEN THE GIRLS were in grade school and did their homework, I worked alongside them, and slowly through the years I improved my reading and writing skills. Even so, I still struggle with feelings of terror when I need to write down things in front of people. What if someone finds me out to be the ignorant person I am? I understand where this fear comes from, and I don't like the feeling, but I no longer let it stop me from doing the things I want to do.

I was constantly trying to learn what I perceived everyone else already knew, and because I couldn't learn it all, I decided I wasn't very smart. I kept trying to learn anyway. I obtained a GED certificate and signed up for college classes.

One day I saw Will Durant on television. They were talking about how his books, *The Story of Civilization* were being translated into different languages. I was interested in the Reformation so I checked that one out of the library. Then I discovered I could get all his books inexpensively in the Book-of-the-Month Club and a whole new world opened up for me. With the dictionary at my side, I worked my way through various parts of all eleven volumes. I found that I love to read philosophy. It cheers me up to no end.

WHILE LIVING in England, I would never have dreamt of becoming a citizen; it was my duty to not like the English. As a child I remember when English people came to visit us in Cork, I'd hear grownups say, "Well they were really nice for being English."

The English felt the same way about the Irish. When St. Patrick's Day approached, my English friends would talk about how all the Irish were going to get drunk and there'd be fighting in the streets. Then they'd

America

remember I was listening and add, "But not you, Maura."

When I got to America, no one said they were American; they were Irish, English Hungarian, or some other nationality. Even Jack's family who'd been in America for generations never called themselves Americans; they referred to their English, Irish, and French heritage when asked. America was a country of immigrants and I embraced it.

While working at the Inverness Hotel as a seamstress in the 1980s, I met many people who emigrated from Mexico and other countries south of the U.S. border. Most of these people were in the country legally; but some were using false documents to work at the hotel. Their stories reminded me of how I, as a young girl, had moved from Ireland to England with a false identity in order to obtain full-time work.

My fellow workers at the Inverness Hotel were hardworking people who saved their money and denied themselves all kinds of things so they could have more money to send home. While working at the hotel, I witnessed the Immigration and Naturalization Service, the INS, conduct two raids looking for undocumented workers. It was horrible for me to watch people take off running like they were criminals. One person tried to hide under the dirty laundry but was found out. The manager of the hotel laundromat, who was several generations American, had to show

An Irish Face

INS his identification. Because my skin was white, no one asked to see my papers. The whole operation seemed ugly and wrong and I was so disturbed by it, I broke down and cried. The INS agent was concerned about me but didn't have a clue why I was so sad.

IT TOOK ME a long time before I become a citizen of the United States. Alanna, my oldest daughter, pushed me to get my Certificate of Naturalization by making a bet with me. She was going to be 18 the following year, and if I became eligible to vote before she did, she would take me out to dinner.

I had already taken all the classes I needed to, but had never gotten around to taking the test. Alanna's bet got me going on the final step, and we had a wonderful time at a nice restaurant down by the beach.

The more I learned, the more threatened Jack became, which only made me more determined to improve myself. I was just as determined my daughters would be educated. I did not want them to live with the fear and shame I'd lived with.

MANY MEN of Jack's generation (including Jack) felt threatened by the women's movement. One evening when the girls were still in high school and middle school, Jack called us all together for a family meeting. He announced he was not going to pay for any of the girls to go to college. If they wanted to continue their education beyond high school, they would have to figure out how to do it on their own.

We were devastated. The girls and I all cried together, but Jack's edict only strengthened my resolve to help our daughters find a way to get through college.

The girls all worked very hard. They got loans, did work-study programs, and held part-time jobs—anything they could do they did—to earn their degrees.

JACK WAS VERY PROUD of all his daughters' accomplishments. When I made plans to go to Pennsylvania to see Lisa present her dissertation for a Ph.D. on the Mars space program, Jack (even though we were separated at the time) came with me.

I learned sometime later from his sister Jo that Jack credited me for pushing our daughters to get an 4education. If he could have said things like that to me instead of calling me wasteful and stupid, how different life would have been.

WHEN JACK WAS promoted to district manager for his company in 1977, we moved to Colorado. Shortly after arriving in Colorado, I enrolled in Barnes Business College. Jack found petty ways to undermine me. He scolded me for doing my homework in the dining room, saying I would leave marks on our good table.

Instead of encouraging me, he pushed me to give up, and he ended up getting his way. I couldn't type the 35 words a minute required to pass the typing test, and I needed a passing grade in typing to graduate. Even though I didn't graduate from business school, I learned a lot from the classes I took so I never felt I wasted my time there.

After the girls were grown and gone, I still held a glimmer of hope that Jack and I could make our marriage work. Sometimes we had great conversations, and I didn't understand why we couldn't just get along. We had enough money, and at times, we had great fun together. Why was this so hard? Why did Jack have to be such a bully?

I REMEMBER WATCHING a Jack Cousteau program on captured dolphins one day. The dolphins were swimming in a small pool with walls all around it. They'd lived in that pool since they were quite small. When they were first introduced to the pen they couldn't have jumped out of it if they'd wanted to. But now they were grown and could easily have leaped over the walls but they didn't even try. *I'm like those dolphins*, I thought. I'm not happy in this marriage, and I could get out of it, but I don't even try.

ONE DAY, when it was just Jack and I living together, and I was bored out of my wits, I went to the cleaners where I took our dry cleaning and told the manager I could sew. I had never done it professionally, but I asked him if he would hire me and he said yes.

I learned how to do alterations, and I loved the work. I continued working there until my grandson, Brad, was born, and then I quit so I could spend more time helping Alanna with the new baby. Poor Alanna. She didn't know what to do with me, but she was very nice about it. I eventually took a part-time job at a men's clothing store doing alterations and waited for Alanna to call me for help. That worked best.

One day, unaware of how close Jack was to losing me, he told me I was lazy. He had called me many awful names through the years, but this was the first time he told me I was lazy. Lazy was the one thing I knew I was not.

That is such a lie, I thought.

ONCE AGAIN, as I had done years before when the children were small, I sat down by myself to re-evaluate my life. What was the worst thing that could happen to me if I left Jack?

I might end up homeless.

Okay....

If I end up having to live on the streets as a homeless person, I will decorate my grocery cart with lace and frills and be the finest bag lady I can be.

It made me laugh just thinking about it. Armed with the knowledge I could survive my worst fears, I was ready to jump out of the pool and into the ocean. Before I jumped, I gave Jack one more chance.

If Jack would go with me to get help with our marriage, I would stay and try to work it out.

He refused.

WHEN I FINALLY broke the news to the girls that I was divorcing their father, Alanna told me she was amazed I hadn't done it earlier. Jack was embarrassed to tell his co-workers his wife was leaving him and he kept our picture on his desk at work. He refused to leave our home so we stayed together for awhile, sleeping in separate bedrooms. Once, in an effort to make up with me, he suggested we work on the park bench I was refinishing for the backyard. I was busy doing something else at the time, and told him I didn't want to work on the fucking bench. It shocked him that I'd speak to him that way, but by this time I didn't care what he thought.

Jack and I lived apart but together for awhile because I wasn't able to move either. I was going to do it tomorrow. Meanwhile, I had this secret ambition to own a Bed and Breakfast someday, so I took a job at the Inverness hotel as a maid. I was quite professional, answering the phone, "Housekeeping, may I help you?" The management liked me so much they let go of their seamstress (whom they didn't like) and put me in that position.

When Alanna and Herman moved to California to take care of his mother, who had been in an auto accident, I finally moved out of the family home and rented their home from them. In 1991 I purchased a townhouse and helped Alanna and Herman sell their home. They returned to Colorado a few years later.

THE ANGER I FELT toward Jack had been building for years and now served as a powerful force that drove me as far away from him as I could get.

I didn't understand what was happening to me at first. I was in this race with time and did everything with great speed. I rushed to get gas in the car, to go here and go there. I couldn't slow down enough to read or watch TV. The pounds fell off me, and that part

I liked, but I didn't like wondering if I was going out of my mind.

At the women's resource center at Arapahoe Community College, I explained my situation to the woman in charge. I was talking a mile a minute; I had so much to say. I didn't know how she understood me, but she did. She set me up with a counselor who worked with me one-on-one for a while. This counselor told me I was suffering from symptoms of depression. Once I knew what was going on, I coped much better. When the counselor started a support group with some other women who were also going through tough times, I joined the group, and stayed with it for many years. To this day I remain friends with the women I met in that group.

Jack and I had dinner together from time to time to talk about the divorce settlement. In small ways I could tell Jack wanted to set things right between us. He brought me flowers and helped me put up curtains in Alanna and Herman's house while I was renting it. When we met for dinner, he acted like we were on a date, but I would have none of it. I was there to talk about the divorce and that was all.

Before the divorce was final, Jack got a mutual friend of ours to ask me if I would come back to him. She never told me Jack was the one asking this, and when I found out later, after he died, it felt like she had betrayed our friendship. I don't know if it would have changed anything for Jack and me, but it changed things between us, and we were never friends after that.

IN EARLY DECEMBER, 1991 it was discovered Jack had spurs on his neck and needed throat surgery. I was suspicious at first that this was only a ruse to delay the divorce. When I realized Jack truly did need surgery, I spent the whole day in Alanna's house by myself with the phone off the hook looking back over my life. I thought and cried the entire day away. If Jack was a stranger to me, and he needed my help, I would help him. There was no reason not to help the man who was the father of my children and the grandfather of their children.

I felt much better once I made the decision to help Jack. I invited him out to breakfast to let him know I'd help him through his surgery, but I would not delay the divorce proceedings. His friend, John, took him to the hospital for the surgery, but Jack asked me to take him home afterwards. He said he couldn't stand John's driving. I agreed to drive him home, and I got him the silk scarf he needed to wear on his neck (other materials were too painful) and some Playboy magazines he wanted.

An Irish Face

THE BITTERNESS I FELT toward Jack lasted long after the divorce was final, and I avoided being around him as much as possible. My grandchild, Nathan, who was about five at the time, helped get me back on the road to forgiveness. After work, I often picked Nathan up on my way home so he could spend a few hours with me.

Nathan was quite chatty, and one day he asked me, "Do you know my Grandpa Jack? You should come to my house and meet him. I think you'd like Grandpa Jack."

I was so embarrassed and ashamed of myself I couldn't say a word. I had been acting like a child in front of this dear boy, and he called me on it. Right then and there, I decided I would change my behavior toward Jack. There was no reason I couldn't exchange pleasantries with him without reliving my grievances, and I didn't need to leave family gatherings early anymore just because Jack was coming.

It took at least another year before I could talk to Nathan about the fact that not only did I know his Grandpa Jack, we were once married. I'm sure he had no idea how hard it was for me to have that conversation with him or what he'd started by his innocent question, "Do you know my Grandpa Jack?"

We gradually became friends again, and one day Jack asked me to have dinner with him. He showed me

America

a brochure of a motor home called a 5th wheel. The front of it fit onto a truck when you were driving down the road, and when you parked it for the night, the living room and bedroom expanded into a small living space. Jack planned to buy one of these trailers and drive around the country with it. When the children were young, we'd talked about doing this zigzag across the country, and now he was going to make it happen.

Jack began a routine where he spent his summers in Denver and in October he headed to California with his 5th wheel for the winter. While he was in Colorado, he came over to my townhouse to visit when the kids and grandkids were there. He swam in the pool at my complex and took walks with me.

One day, Jack called to tell me his nephew had died at the age of 49. Gary was Bette's son, and we were all very close. Bette and her family had lived down the block from us in Whittier, California when our children were growing up. I told Jack I was going to the funeral. Jack got us both airline tickets. He parked his truck in my garage, and we drove my car to the airport and flew together to the funeral in Napa. That was our first trip together after the divorce, and it went well. We shared a room, and he kissed me hello and good bye. He was on his best behavior.

The next year, Jack invited me to travel to Redding with him in his trailer. I drove out with him for a short visit and then came home on the train, while he stayed on in California. On that trip, Jack (he couldn't seem to help himself) occasionally lapsed into moments of ugliness that served to remind me why I'd left him.

I went with Jack to California a few more times. On each visit his behavior toward me improved, and I found it easier to get along with him. One trip I planned to stay with Bette in California, but he asked me to stay with him, and I agreed to do so. It was an old habit of mine to always go along if it made other people happy. The truth was, I didn't mind spending time with Jack as long as I didn't have to live with him.

WHEN OUR GRANDAUGHTER Rachel was five, Jack came back from California not looking well. He thought he might have suffered a mild stroke. He'd been out to the bar with his friend, John, and when he got up from the bar stool, his legs gave out. We were at Rachel's birthday party at Park Meadows, and I noticed he looked different somehow, very strained. He told me he was having trouble with his feet.

Alanna told him of a walk-in clinic he could go to, and I said I'd go with him. The next day I called Jack to see what time he wanted to go to the clinic, and he said he couldn't talk right now; he was brushing his teeth. Then he hung up.

Something was terribly wrong. Jack couldn't be brushing his teeth; the only teeth he had by then were false teeth.

I waited awhile, then drove over to his place and told him I would buy him lunch before we went to the clinic.

Jack insisted on driving. We had lunch and then headed for the clinic, but Jack didn't have the address and we got lost. He got very nasty with me until I shouted at him that he could take me home if that's how it was going to be.

I think he knew he was very sick and really didn't want to know what was wrong with him.

Somehow, we found the clinic and got Jack's head and lungs x-rayed. Once that was done, Jack felt more relaxed, and we went outside so he could smoke a cigarette. The Physician's Assistant came outside to find us, and said to Jack, "I should tell you to stop smoking but your lungs are fine. We have to find where the mass on your brain is coming from." She then told Jack he needed to see a cancer specialist right away. The cancer specialist was very busy, and the only way Jack could see her on such short notice was to check into the hospital that night, and she would see him on her rounds in the morning.

Lisa came over that night, and we had dinner

An Irish Face

together. Jack was grateful to have us with him. The next day he found out he had cancer and would need to spent time in the hospital undergoing radiation treatment. The source of his cancer was never found.

Jack had been living in his trailer at Flying Saucer Trailer Park on Hampden and Federal, but he soon discovered he could no longer handle the steps. I thought long and hard about what to do. Jack hated being in the hospital, but he needed someone to take care of him. Our girls were busy with family and careers. I was the only one who had the time to care for him, but could I bring myself to do it? Once again, I came to the conclusion; if Jack were a stranger who needed help I would help him.

When I told Jack he could leave the hospital and come home with me, he thanked me. Hospice helped me set up a hospital bed in my living room where he stayed until he died. The kids and grandkids came around in the evenings to visit and watch television with him. I knew he appreciated all I did for him once I brought him home with me, but he couldn't tell me so.

Jack could not talk about the fact that he was dying. Instead, he spent his last days focusing on getting stronger. He kept asking for physical therapy long after there was no hope of his getting well again. The physical therapist who came to the house gently told him that it was a good thing he wanted to get stronger but right now he needed to use all his energy to get well. She took him into the kitchen and taught him how to pull himself up by holding on to the kitchen sink and he was grateful for that. When Alanna came over, he couldn't wait to show her what he could do.

At the end of his life Jack couldn't say he was sorry, and he couldn't say goodbye, but he could and often did say, "I love you" to our children and grandchildren.

Despite his many flaws, I knew he loved us.

One day after the divorce was final, Jack came to me with an envelope stuffed with papers. He'd had a meeting with the girls, and it hadn't gone well. He had a habit of saying the wrong thing, and he said something in the middle of the meeting that made Alanna get up in disgust and walk out. Jack told me the bulky papers in the envelope were for the girls, and he wanted me to keep them. I didn't ask him anything about the papers nor did I look at them after he left. I took the envelope to the bank and put it in the safety deposit box.

Jack named Alanna as the executor of his will, and she confided in me that she wanted to include me in her father's inheritance. I told her no. We'd split the property when we divorced; what he left behind belonged to his daughters. After Jack died, we got the envelope from the safety deposit box and read his Last Will and Testament. That is when we discovered Jack wanted his inheritance to be divided five ways between his four daughters and me.

I'm grateful I didn't know he'd done this when I made the decision to help him while he was dying. I would hate to think my decision to bring him home with me was colored by the fact I was going to inherit money from him. Because I didn't know what was in the envelope, I never had to question my motives.

I had made the decision to help Jack at the end of his life because it was the right thing to do.

Part Four

On My Own

The beginning of wisdom is: get wisdom; at the cost of all you have, get understanding.
　　　　　　　Proverbs 4, *American Standard Bible*

An Irish Face

I visited Ireland and England in July 2005 with my daughters: Alanna, Zana, and Lisa, my grandchildren: Brad, Lauren, Nathan, and Rachel, and my son-in-law, Herman. We spent a weekend in England and then left for two weeks in Ireland.

On My Own

While in London, we stayed in Russell Square and used the tube to get around. We were traveling in Ireland when we got the news that terrorists had bombed four different places in London. One of the blasts occurred between Russell Square and the King's Cross tube stations where we'd been just the week before.

During our visit, I noticed the language differences amongst my relatives who never left Ireland or England. While visiting Cork, I listened to two young people who seemed to be conversing in a foreign language but soon realized they were speaking English with a thick Irish brogue.

In Cork, the *th* sound is not used. Thunder sounds like *tunder*, think becomes *tink* and that is *dat*. When I was young and did manage to attend school, the teachers worked on us to pronounce the *th* sound properly. I remember Annie had a friend we admired because she pronounced the *th* sound so well.

Some of my nephews and nieces raised in London speak with a strong British accent. When we visited the London Tower, the guard at the tower could tell where my niece, Delia, lived in London by her Cockney accent.

I love spending time with my niece Delia, Kittie's daughter. She was named Bridget, but we call her Delia. Because the Irish keep reusing names (Mary,

Bridget Kathleen, etc.) few of us are known by our given names. Often times, the familiar name has no connection to the given name, and it sometimes catches me by surprise to hear what a person's real name is after years of calling them something different.

    Delia is the keeper of the family stories in England. Her generation's childhood stories are not much happier than mine were and from what Annie and Kittie used to tell me about our grandmother, Mother's childhood couldn't have been easy either. Mother learned to do things out of a sense of duty, rather than kindness. The lack of food and money seemed to make her stingy in other ways too. She didn't find people interesting like I did. When visitors came to our house, they fascinated me with their stories. When they left I was eager to know more about them, but Mother only took pleasure in ridiculing them and telling me what fools they were.

    After Jack and I separated, one of the assignments I had in group therapy was to think of a time when I was happy with my parents. It shocked me that I couldn't think of one loving memory of Mother and me alone together. The closest I could come to a pleasant memory was a time when Mother, Annie, Kittie, and I went on a walk and we talked and laughed together. It was a brief, peaceful moment in time.

On My Own

OVER THE YEARS I learned I could get information about my biological mother and track down my original family if I wanted to, but until recently I was reluctant to do so. I'd thought about the woman who gave birth to me all my life. As a child I fantasized she would come and save me from the poverty we lived in. When my friend Peggy got pregnant out of wedlock, kept her child and lovingly reared her, I thought, how could she do it and my mother couldn't? I had to remind myself that in 1935 when I was born, Ireland was a brand-new nation coming out of such poverty that good heavens, it was a wonder we survived at all.

During the Civil Rights Movement in the 60s, I didn't search for my birth family because I didn't want anything to jeopardize the sense of belonging I had with the world. It didn't matter where I came from; I knew I belonged to this world just the way I was.

I've often told people I'm a tree with no roots but lots of branches. That isn't exactly true. My roots are in Ireland and England, in both the family I grew up with and the family I never met.

I think of Ireland as my parents but America is my home.

In the spring of 2008, with the help of my daughter Zana, we wrote to the nuns of Sacred Heart, requesting information about my first mother. The information we received did not match the stories my sisters and mother told me. I discovered my natural mother was not the young woman I'd imagined, nor did she work for a doctor, nor was it my father who paid for my mother's keep in the convent.

On May 6, 2008, Sr. Mary McManus sent the following email to Zana:

> It was the Catholic Woman's Aid Society that placed your mother Mary with Mrs. Moore. This was a private fostering arrangement and Mary's mother paid for the care of Mary up until January 1938.
>
> The Catholic Woman's Aid Society (CWAS) was one of the first Roman Catholic agencies to arrange fostering/adoption for children before adoption was made legal in Ireland in 1952. Mrs. Crowe was the founding member of the society.
>
> We hold some of the CWAS records.
>
> We can tell you from that, Mary's mother was also Mary O'Sullivan. Mary gave two addresses when she was admitted to Bessborough. The first address was Mary O'Sullivan, Dreenaverrissry, Caheragh, Drimaleague, Co. Cork (West Cork.) The second was

a convenience address used for many of the girls. Mary gave her age as 39 to be 40 in February 1935.

Her occupation is given as general maid with a Teacher in West Cork. Wage £14 per year. She was educated at Killeenigh National School, the records do not say to what standard. Her parents were dead and she had one brother.

We have had no enquiry about your mother or grandmother. It is very possible that nobody was aware that she was pregnant and came here.

I found the news from Ireland unsettling. It was easy to feel compassion for a young woman without the means to keep a child who was taken advantage of by a man who had power over her. I now had to learn compassion for a 40-year-old woman who left me to be raised by another woman who had no more money than she did at the time of my birth.

Sr. Mary McManus's email gave me more unanswered questions than I had before. Who was my father? Was he the teacher my mother worked for or someone else? Why didn't my father marry my mother? When Mother saw Mary O'Sullivan on the bus, she had to have known how old she was. Why did Mother lead me to believe my first mother was a young girl?

An Irish Face

The story of my birth has changed again but the truth remains the same. Because of the terrible shame of unwed pregnancy, my natural mother hid in a convent until my birth and left me to be raised by another woman.

My mother, due to whatever the circumstances of my conception were, could not celebrate my birth as I have been so fortunate to celebrate the births of all my children and grandchildren.

After all these years, there is still so much I don't understand about myself, including the part of me that hurts so much sometimes. I don't understand it; but then maybe I'm not supposed to. I do know that when I lean into the sorrow and accept this part of life for what it is, it opens me up to the joy that waits on the other side.

THE BEST PART OF MY LIFE was becoming a mother and my greatest fear, raising my children, was that I would do the wrong thing. I worried constantly about it. I took parenting classes, attended lectures, and read books on parenting in order to become a better mother.

There were times the girls would catch me off guard. They were so close in age, they could wear each other's clothes and they often did; all they had to do was ask. One time Zana and Michelle got into a big fight.

On My Own

I can't remember who borrowed who's sweater but one of them came to me complaining bitterly that the other one had borrowed her clothes without asking. I reminded them of the rule, "You have to ask if you want to wear someone's clothes."

"Can I borrow your sweater?"

"No!"

Now what am I supposed to do?

SHUT UP was a real swear word to me. Growing up, I had a friend whose brother said it constantly, and it really annoyed me. I didn't want my children to be like that, so I wouldn't allow them to say it to each other.

The girls hated it when I lectured them about what they should or shouldn't do. They'd roll their eyes and beg me to stop. I remember once they were teasing me, and said they'd rather get hit or slapped than endure another of my long lectures; it was just about the worse punishment they could get.

I insisted, "No, no, you have to listen to me," but they didn't want to hear it.

One time I overheard Lisa talking to her friend on the telephone, and I thought, *that can't be my daughter.* She was consoling and advising her friend using something she'd heard from me. Who knew? Some of what I was trying to say was getting through after all.

WHEN THE CHILDREN were very young, I attended a lecture at the library by the school psychologist, and she explained there were all kinds of love: romantic, sisterly, sibling, friendship, and the unconditional love you have for your children.

The love you have for your children is unlike the love you have for anyone else. What people do to you can alter your feelings toward them, but it doesn't work like that with your babies. They throw up on you, they pee on you, and it's all fine; it doesn't change how you feel about them. I was delighted to hear this woman put into words what I had been feeling toward my children all along.

When my daughters were born, I was astonished at the love I had for them. The fact that I was capable of loving all of them equally and unconditionally was one of the greatest discoveries in my life.

Once when my daughter Zana was playing jump rope with a friend and I was talking on the telephone, she decided to use the end table to hold down one end of the rope. When she lifted up the table, the lamp fell and broke. She looked at me, terrified. It scared me to see her so afraid of me. What the heck, it was only a broken lamp. What kind of monster did she think I was? Because of that incident I went to the girls' school and asked for help. I did not want my children to be afraid of me like that.

On My Own

During group therapy I broke down and cried. The leader took me aside and said, "Sometimes it's pretty hard to love your child."

"No, that's not it. She's so easy to love, that's not my problem," I said. I remember how surprised he was; it wasn't what he was expecting to hear at all.

I used the incident with Zana and the broken lamp to join the group, but it was for all my children that I attended the parenting class. When I was growing up, Mother loved to favor one of us over the others to make the rest feel jealous, and it was very important I not be that kind of mother. I wanted all my children to feel as special as Aunt Biddie made me feel when I was growing up, and I did whatever I could to make that happen.

To be the kind of mother I had wanted for myself when I was a child—that was my guide. At times I could see I wasn't necessarily the kind of mother each of my four children wanted, but it was the best I had to offer.

It seems silly now, but when Alanna gave birth to Bradley, my first grandchild, I worried she might not be a good mother to her son. Of course she was. When I told her once how glad I was she was such a good mother she said to me, "Why wouldn't I be? I had a good mother."

That pleased me to no end.

An Irish Face

Maura with her daughters, 2007
Left to right: Zana, Michelle, Alanna, and Lisa

As a child, I hated having to be grateful, but now I find myself filled with gratitude. The joy I've experienced in life balances the pain I carry with me from childhood. The smallest thing—whether it's a beautiful flower, a blue sky, a nice sunset, or even a pleasant exchange with a stranger—reminds me that beauty is everywhere if I choose to see it.

On My Own

Maura with her grandchildren, 2009
Left to right: Lauren, Brad, Nathan and Rachael

I wish my original mother could have known what she started over three quarters of a century ago in Ireland.

Because she gave birth to me, this world is blessed with four lovely women and four beautiful grandchildren who enrich our planet by their very presence.

For everything that went into making me the woman I am today, I am grateful.

Life is good. It's all good.

Epilogue

Life Goes On

The motto for the O'Sullivans is "An Lámh Fhoisteanach Abú" which translates as "The Steady Hand to Victory".
http://en.wikipedia.org/wiki/O%27Sullivan

An Irish Face

*I*n 2010, when Maura's daughter Lisa, honeymooned in Ireland with her husband David, they explored the area of County Cork where Maura's biological mother lived. Using the information provided by Sister Mary McManus, and with some help from the local people who gave them the correct spelling of places mentioned in Sister's email, they tracked down a tombstone in the Caheragh Old Burial Ground that seemed to fit what little information they had regarding Maura's family of birth. According to Sister McManus, when Mary gave birth to Maura, Mary's parents were dead, but she had a brother who was still alive.

Epilogue

>In
>Loving Memory Of
>MICHAEL O'SULLIVAN
>DREENAVERIHY
>DIED 27 MARCH 1982.
>HIS WIFE NORA
>DIED 1. AUG. 1947.
>HIS SISTERS
>MARY. DIED 28. AUG. 1955.
>JANE. DIED 28. AUG. 1955.

It wasn't until the following year that Maura's family could confirm this was indeed Maura's mother in the cemetery. In June 2011, Maura, Lisa, Alanna, Herman, and Delia (Maura's niece from London) traveled the country roads that lead to the Caheragh Old Burial Ground. They got lost along the way and stopped at a farmhouse to get directions. Instead of directing them to the cemetery, the woman they talked to sent them to the O'Sullivan farm on Derreenavarrihy road where Sullivans[8] have resided for five generations.

Upon arrival at the farm, they were warmly greeted by Maureen, wife of Jerry O'Sullivan, the current owner of

---

[8] O'Sullivan (Irish Ó Súileabháin or Ó Súilleabháin) or simply Sullivan is an Irish surname, associated with the southwestern part of Ireland, originally found in County Tipperary before the Anglo-Norman invasion, then in County Cork and County Kerry, which due to emigration is also common in Australia, North America and Britain. The O'Sullivans are the medieval and modern continuation of the ancient Eóganacht Chaisi sept of Cenél Fíngin, being descendants of Fíngen mac Áedo Duib, king of Cashelor Munster from 601 to 618. They are thus understood to be of royal extraction. Fedelmid mac Crimthainn (died 847), the celebrated King of Munster and nearly High King of Ireland, was the last king of the Cenél Fíngin/O'Sullivan line. Later they became the chief princes underneath their close kinsmen the MacCarthy dynasty in the small but powerful Kingdom of Desmond, successor of Cashel/Munster.

In the last 200 or 300 years those families connected to the name have dispersed widely throughout the English-speaking world and to other areas. Emigrants often suppressed the prefix "O".

In the Irish language the word Ó means 'grandson' and can be found in many Irish surnames. It has been anglicised as O'. When placed before the genitive form of Súileabhán, which is Súileabháin, it can be translated as grandson of. While the use of an apostrophe is a common convention in English, the apostrophe is never used in the original Irish language version of the name....

http://en.wikipedia.org/wiki/O%27Sullivan

Epilogue

the farm. Jerry's father was Michael O'Sullivan, who was buried with his wife, Nora, and his sisters, Mary and Jane, in the Caheragh Old Burial Ground under the tombstone Lisa and David had discovered earlier.

Maura explained to Maureen the purpose of their visit. She told Maureen she wasn't there to cause a disturbance, but she had reason to believe she was related to the Sullivans through Mary who died in 1955. She assured Maureen she'd understand if no one at the farm wanted to talk to her; Maura could very well be an old secret her mother took to the grave with her.

Without hesitation, Maureen told Maura that some years earlier, Jerry's uncle, when he was a bit tipsy, asked Jerry, "Did you know your Auntie Mary had a baby girl?"

Maureen invited Maura and her family in, and then called Jerry away from his work on the farm to come home and meet his long-lost cousin Maura. Maureen and Jerry shared pictures from their family photograph album with Maura and her family. Maureen did most of the talking, but when Jerry did say something, he spoke with a thick brogue, and Maura had a hard time understanding him. It didn't seem to matter though; Maura remembers the time she spent with the O'Sullivans as a delightful afternoon of conversation and laughter.

Maura at the O'Sullivan farm
A picture of Maura's grandparents, Julia and Jeremiah, is on the floor next to her.

After Maura and her family left the O'Sullivans, they drove to the cemetery where Maura's original mother was buried.

Maura was 20 years old at the time of Mary's death on August 28, 1955. It was the summer Maura met Jack and applied for a job in America. In November of that year, the letter arrived from the reverend Mother of Sacred Heart

Epilogue

Hospital that sent Maura into a fit of weeping like nothing she'd ever experienced before or since.

THROUGH A GENEOLIGIST at the Skibbereen Heritage Center, Lisa obtained baptismal certificates for Julia and Jeremiah Sullivan (Maura's grandparents), Mary (Maura's mother) and Michael, Daniel, and Jane, (Maura's uncles and aunt.) Lisa also found the Sullivans listed in the 1901 and 1911 Census records, the only two complete Censuses available in Ireland.

According to the records found, Mary was 44 years old when she gave birth to Maura—not 40 as she told the Sisters of Sacred Heart.

Maura was born on February 11, 1935, but she and her mother were not discharged from Bessboro until April 1, 1935. It is not known how much contact Maura and her mother had with each other in that short period of time.

MAURA ONCE DESCRIBED to me this mental image she had of a hole in her heart. It looked like a geode with color all around it and a very dark center. Shortly after her latest visit to Ireland in 2011, while sitting in her living room thinking about her trip, Maura experienced a great sense of release from all the unanswered questions about her mother over the years, and she felt the hole close up.

"It's a hole that has always been there and now it's just gone," she said.

An Irish Face

I MET MAURA in 2003, the same year she saw the movie, The Magdalene Sisters. *We were both learning how to play bridge. Although I don't remember anything about the bridge class, I'll never forget how Maura put me at ease when she invited me to join her table. During the play of the hand, when I hesitated, afraid I'd make a mistake, she laughed and said, "Go on! It's just a game."*

From the very beginning of our friendship, I was drawn to Maura's melodic laugh and relaxed attitude, not only about bridge, but this thing we call life. When Maura casually mentioned to me once that she was born in a convent in Ireland, I wanted to know more.

What roads had Maura traveled before she showed up at bridge class and invited me to play? What went into making her the confident and delightful woman I knew?

The stories Maura shared with me on the pages of this book explain a lot about who Maura is and the journey she is on, but there will always be unanswered questions.

How did Maura's first mother, Mary O'Sullivan, live the remaining 20 years of her life with the pain of letting go of her only child? Who fathered Maura? Why didn't Maura's parents marry and keep her? Was their union consensual?

The circumstances surrounding Maura's conception may never be known, but one (of many) things Maura has taught me over the years, is when you embrace the mystery of life, it allows you to let go of the need to know everything.

Epilogue

MARY O'SULLIVAN, because she was an unwed mother in 1935, could not openly celebrate the birth of her daughter. But because she gave the gift of life to her child, the rest of us who know and love Maura have been celebrating ever since.

Which brings me to another question. Of all the bridge classes in all of Denver, why did Maura walk into mine?

Whatever the reason, I'm glad she did.

As Maura often says, "Life is good. It's all good."

△△△

Acknowlegements

I am deeply grateful to the following people who reviewed this book and gave advice on various aspects of it prior to publication: Jack Keane, Patricia Cox, Sharon Mohatt, Zana Brown, Lisa Riley Brown, and of course Maura O'Sullivan, herself.

Without their encouragement and the generous donation of their time, this book would still be just an idea in my head.

Angela Keane, a member of the Denver Woman's Press Club, lives in Colorado with her husband and two dogs. She writes, edits, and publishes personal memoirs through Story Preserves.

Made in the USA
Charleston, SC
01 March 2014